# TIME FOR A NEW KING

BENJAMIN MARSHALL

All rights reserved. No part of this book may be reproduced in any form or by any means without permission in writing from the publisher.

Printed in the United States of America
Publisher Address

©2019 Benjamin Marshall

Edited by Okorie Godsmight
Cover image and design by: charlyn_designs@fiverr.com

ISBN: 978-0-9729904-1-7

Unless otherwise indicated all Scripture quotations are taken from the King James Version of the Bible

Author contact: tellthetruthsac@gmail.com

I dedicate this first work of many to:

Bernice Marshall
*(Late paternal grandmother)*
and

Grover Talley
*(Late maternal grandfather)*

I miss them.
Both recently passed after living a very long,
blessed life. Their commitment to God,
legacy, love, and prayers for me,
has no doubt helped me get this far.

# CONTENTS

Acknowledgements ................................................... 7
Introduction ............................................................... 9

Chapter 1:   Promise Kept ..................................... 13
Chapter 2:   My Throne ........................................ 20
Chapter 3:   Attempted Takeover ......................... 29
Chapter 4:   Man As King ..................................... 38
Chapter 5:   What Is Truth? .................................. 48
Chapter 6:   Wise Men ........................................... 57
Chapter 7:   Religion Vs Kingdom ........................ 65
Chapter 8:   King And Wealth ............................... 72
Chapter 9:   Kingdom Rules .................................. 83
Chapter 10: King Of Hearts ................................. 102
Chapter 11: Kingdom Invasion ............................ 112
Chapter 12: It's Time ............................................ 123

# ACKNOWLEDGEMENTS

First of all, to my children, Trevaughn, Brianna, Benjamin, and Josiah who are extremely important to me, I love you. You taught me so much about being a father and helped me to realize how much I needed my Heavenly Father in order to be a good father for you.

My mom, Helen Talley and my dad, Oliver Marshall, have always believed in me and supported me every step of the way. I honor you both.

Apostle Ricky Nutt & Pastor George Brown. Thank you for believing and investing in me.

My dearest friends, always there to pray, support me, and speak words of life: Johnny Jones, Richard Balian, Bruce Twamley, Jacqueline Ball, and Ma and Pa Banks, who are my biggest fans.

My church family and international family in Liberia, Haiti, and Kenya; thank you for your love and support.

# INTRODUCTION

There comes a time when one comes to realize that it is completely up to them as to what happens to them - at least for the most part. It is probably safe to say, most of us have heard and can agree to the philosophy that says, "I decide my own fate. I have to solve my own problems. I have to make it happen for myself. I control what happens with me. I must make and live with the decisions I made in my past, make in my present, and will make in my future."

In speaking to you through the pages of this book, it would seem foolish to argue against this. The truth that this carries leaves little doubt that it is in your hands to a large extent what your destiny becomes. You were created as a freewill being. You were given the ability under God's supervision to create, make, and speak regarding the quality of your existence. You have free choice as to what route you will take, and there is no disagreement there. However, this is not the complete truth. A huge element is missing that must be disclosed and discussed.

In all of this, I have come to understand; there are some things you can control and other things out of your control. More importantly, there are some things you can control that you are not supposed to. Do you know the difference? Can you identify what those things are? Also, you have options regarding the method you use to get where you want to go. Do you know what they are? How much thought have you given to them?

There is a thought I would like us to consider as we explore the idea of control. The question, "Who are we?" is significant to it. Where did we come from? Who are we responsible to? These questions are even more important. Even though I may have been taught and believed that I am the king of my life, my world, and my future and the one to make the ultimate decisions concerning what happens to me, there is yet a sobering truth that must be confronted: We are created. We are not self-made. We have been made by someone else. We are limited. You and I don't sit on the top alone. There is a top above our top.

This brings me to the idea of accountability and responsibility. I am accountable and responsible to someone else for my actions. You are as well. I am not my own authority whether I want to accept that or not. I operate my life under someone else's authority; whether I realize it or not. The buck doesn't stop here with me after all.

The thought of kingship is humbling and also challenging. If indeed I am not the self-proclaimed king I thought I was or have been made to believe; how do I accept and deal with this? Who is my king? What does he want? What am I now responsible for?

Identifying and accepting the true king is what this book is all about. There is one greater than us who makes the claim of being King of all kings. He is not a king of force, however. This King has come to take His rightful place at the center of man's being. Yet He does not insist with aggression but appeals to everyone lovingly, kindly, and with patience and truth.

He has already announced His kingship and gives everyone an opportunity by free will to acknowledge His superiority. For centuries, this has been the case with the response of some being full of gratitude and totally receptive; while many others have thoroughly been offended and rejected Him.

Whether it is ego, pride, envy, or ambition that blinds the masses from accepting the claim regarding the existence of a greater king and kingdom, the offer is still continually made available to all during their life on earth. The following pages allow us to look at various stories that challenge us with the truth of the one true King, how mankind relates to this fact, and the results of their decision.

CHAPTER 1

# PROMISE KEPT

*Simeon took him in his arms and praised God, saying: Lord, now you are letting your servant depart in peace, according to your promise, for my eyes have seen your salvation.*

*Luke 2:28-30*

It was God's appointed time to send the Savior to the earth. The season for Him to appear on the scene was now. Much had happened on the earth before that time, and it was now necessary for the heart of God to be revealed through His son to mankind. There were many things that led up to this particular time: the fall of man, the promise given of redemption, and the prophecies spoken by the prophets of old. The stage was now set for these prophecies to be fulfilled.

This promise was to come in the form of a child. The prophecy given over four hundred years earlier to Isaiah reveals this, "For unto us a child is born and a son given. The government shall be on his shoulders and he shall be called Wonderful Counselor, the Mighty God, the Everlasting Father, and Prince of Peace" (Isaiah 9:6).

This was to be no ordinary birth. From the very outset, the circumstances were unlike anything else. We have an engaged couple named Mary and Joseph. She was quiet, shy, and young and he was a devout, God-fearing tradesman of carpentry. What started as a normal story during their time, ended as some describe: *The greatest story that's ever been told.*

One day Mary gets a visit from an angel telling her that she will be with child. Perplexed by this abrupt message, she is trying to understand how this will happen without sexual relations. She is told that what will be born of her is of God. God will be responsible for placing this child in her womb. Joseph doesn't buy this story when he finds out Mary is pregnant. I don't know how anyone would. Yet while contemplating how to leave his seemingly unfaithful partner, he receives a visit by God in a dream. It appears the Lord verifies Mary's story to him.

## TIME FOR A NEW KING

When Mary is around nine months pregnant, they must go register for the census in Nazareth, their hometown. While there, she delivers this promised child in the stall where the animals rest, next to the fully booked inn. She wraps Him tightly with a thick cloth and puts Him in a feeding trough.

Shepherds, while at work, leave to visit Him after having been told by angels of his birth. Wise men coming from afar, also visit Him in this place after having been shown a special star that would assist them in finding Him. What a seemingly strange, unorthodox way to bring the Savior and one who will claim to be the King onto the scene of human history.

It is now time for His parents to take Him to the temple for ceremonial reasons; as the Jewish custom required them to circumcise and dedicate Him at the temple. It is here during this event that a man named Simeon comes and asks for the child. He has been waiting faithfully in expectation of what God had promised him.

Simeon was a man that was a real, true worshipper of God living in Jerusalem. He went about doing what was right to the best of his ability. He was in search of God's answer for His people, Israel.

The Holy Spirit was with him, and God had made him a promise that he would live to see God's answer, the Savior of the world. Not knowing exactly when this would happen, he went about continually living righteously and following God daily. One particular day, he was moved by the Spirit to enter the temple at the same time Jesus and his parents brought him there. When Simeon saw Him, he knew who He was by the Spirit of God. He took him into his arms, blessing, praising, and thanking God. He spoke out, "I can die now in peace because your servant has had the promise you made to him fulfilled."

Before time began, a King had been prepared. Through prophets of old, God had promised a Savior, Messiah, and King. This was not only a promise made and kept for Simeon, but for all Israel and the world. Simeon spoke as a representative, while Jesus parents stood there in amazement of what had been said. Simeon's declaration about God's revelation and salvation for Jews and Gentiles alike was very purposeful.

God always has a witness on the earth confirming what He has established for mankind. God does nothing on the earth without revealing His plans to His holy servants, the prophets (Amos 3:7). The scriptures also teach us that every word is established by the mouth of two or three witnesses (2 Corinthians 13:1). In this case, Simeon is only one of several: the prophets, wise men, shepherds, Mary, and a lady named Anna also joined him.

Anna was a woman totally devoted to God just like Simeon and knew as a result of her prayer to God that a King was coming. She was also promised she would see Him before she left the earth. Anna was seeking God for His redemption and saw it right before her eyes. At that moment this prophetess, who continually sought the Lord, spoke to all around her that He was the redemption Israel awaited (Luke 2:28).

Mary, His mother, was told herself from the angel that she would give birth to the Savior of the world. Her husband Joseph was also told by an angel in a dream that his wife shall bring forth a son and his name would be Jesus for He shall save His people from their sins (Matthew 1:21). The prophecies, given by God to the prophets hundreds of years before, were made with undeniable accuracy; detailing even the very places where these events would take place and what will be done.

These are just some of the many promises made, and all kept to each one of these people. They were all promises made and kept by God Himself. When this

Savior, Deliverer, and King was born, He fulfilled the promises He made to Abraham, Isaac, Jacob, and all their descendants.

Simeon was looking for what was promised to all of us. Are you looking for the same? This promise was also made to you. The promise that this Ruler and King would come to take His rightful place in anyone who accepts Him. God never breaks His promises; He can't because it would go against His nature. He always keeps His promises.

Deuteronomy 7:9 says, "He keeps His covenant with those who love Him for thousands of generations." 2 Timothy 2:13 says, "He remains faithful when we are faithless because He can't deny Himself." And Numbers 23:19 states, "God is not a man that He should lie, or a son of man, that He should change his mind." We know that His word is forever settled in Heaven (Psalms 119:89).

A promise was made because a promise was needed. Hope was needed. A seemingly hopeless situation was set forth, and a fix was necessary. The whole world was in trouble because a wicked kingdom had taken charge that would need to be overthrown. A king and kingdom of light was made known to battle and defeat this kingdom of darkness.

The timing of God's revealed purpose and manifestations are always in His hand, not ours. In our hands is the power to believe, respond, and prepare ourselves. The hour of visitation was chosen, and the time to accept has been given and is currently available to be taken advantage of by all. It is now your turn to accept or reject it. What will you do?

CHAPTER 2

# MY THRONE

*Now when Jesus was born in Bethlehem of Judaea in the days of Herod the king, behold there came wise men from the east to Jerusalem, saying, Where is he that is born King of the Jews? For we have seen his star in the east, and are come to worship him. When Herod the king had heard these things, he was troubled, and all Jerusalem with him.*

Matthew 2:1-2

The reigning earthly king of Judea during that time was a man named King Herod. This man Herod had been appointed the ruling governor of the Jews by the senate in Rome under the kingship of Caesar. He was also known as Herod the Great and his time of ruling, which actually began thirty-seven years before the birth of Christ, was sometimes referred to as the Herodian kingdom. He was known for his colossal building projects throughout Judea and was responsible for the building of the second temple in Jerusalem known to many as Herod's temple.

Here was a man that was focused on making his name great. He did this at the expense of everyone else. People paid heavy taxes under his regime. He was a man that would keep his own position at any cost. The king was a tyrant, seeing to his own cause while exercising his authority with complete domination and control; destroying anyone or anything that would get in his path. He refused to allow anything that would even appear to jeopardize his seat of authority.

Herod King of Judea had heard about a newborn King and was disturbed. Herod decided to seek out the professionals who studied the laws of Israel for research and investigation on this matter of a king to be born. After the wise men shared about their journey to find him, Herod told them to let him know once they located this child. He made it seem like he wanted to take part in the welcoming festivities. As the story goes, the wise men after finding and worshiping the child were warned in a dream by God to exit the country through a different way and not to tell Herod, whose real intention was to destroy this promised King.

Why was Herod so troubled about this baby boy to be born? It wasn't the baby that scared him, but what this baby was prophesied to become; another king. Basically, any king or leader for that matter posed a threat to his kingship and this included future coming kings. Any conversation, or anticipation of anything that might threaten his ruler-ship had to be stopped immediately. Herod took this prophecy seriously, and he would take no chances.

Herod knew that no two kings could rule at the same time. From the moment he heard the news, it was an unwelcomed threat. The very talk of it must be squashed. There would absolutely be no competition here. And this reported future king living in his jurisdiction, must not even have the chance of living and taking part in any ruling conversation at all.

Herod understood what many people fail to realize, that there can never be two kings at one time on the same throne; it's impossible. This new King named Jesus made it impossible because of His declaration as the Son of God, the true King for all mankind. One must be removed because the threat is too much for both to coexist. A king can never rule his province when another is constantly around challenging his throne; therefore, the other one must be silenced by removal, and this removal must be permanent. A king must ensure there will never again be a challenge to his throne. This means death not only to the competitor but also to his lineage. There must not even be an attempt later on. All possibilities must be removed forever. This is seen repeatedly throughout the Bible and in World History.

One of the most ancient ways in the history of ridding yourself of an opponent, especially in the pursuit of having ultimate power, is to assassinate them. The earliest governments and tribes used this method. One of the most famous include Galius Julius Caesar of the Roman Empire. In Russia five emperors were assassinated. In our country we have had four presidents assassinated.

In scripture, Queen Athaliah in Israel became head after killing what she believed to be all the king's family, seventy sons, after his death. King Nebuchadnezzar after capturing Israel killed all of King Zedekiah's sons and government officials, sparing only King Zedekiah by putting out his eyes and imprisoning him until his own death.

Herod would attempt the same. He would rid himself of his supposed enemy by murder. However, he became furious when he realized his deception didn't work with the Wise Men. He then gave orders to kill every male born in the area from the time of the Wise Men's visit. Why? Herod couldn't stomach the idea that someone else greater had come.

Herod, with his own secret plan of destruction, had been out-planned by God though. His chosen King had arrived, and nothing Herod or anyone else tried to do could change it. He would not be removed. In Herod's best effort, he failed.

On the other hand, we are also told that everyone else in the kingdom was bothered as well. Was Jerusalem troubled because the king was troubled? No doubt some were, but I believe they were just troubled themselves. They were concerned about what this meant for them, not just him.

Herod was not a popular king. He was an extension of Rome who Israel was subservient to. Although they were waiting for a Savior for Israel, a promised Messiah that would rule forever; they were probably concerned about how all this would happen.

Many years before, when Moses was sent by God to deliver the children of Israel; at the beginning, the people did not believe him. Later, they rejoiced, and then they were upset with him because of the discomforts they had to endure on their way to freedom. In Israel's mind hearing about a Messiah would probably bring about these same emotions. Is this really happening? Will there be a war? How will we be affected? Will our Messiah be strong enough to defeat the Romans? Will we finally be an independent, autonomous kingdom again? I want you to imagine the talk. Who is this new King and how will He rule us? What will He be like?

What Israel had experienced from being under Roman rule was not good; however, the unknown scared them more. They were afraid and excited at the same time. They were having thoughts of having a better life, yet the fear of what it might cost them.

Are you like Herod or are you more like the Jews? Or are you afraid of both? The replacement of your throne and the fear of the cost it will take to make your life better. It can be both hopeful and scary.

In the same way, Herod resisted the talk of a new King, who he assumed would replace him on the throne. We have a natural human tendency to resist any talk of a person who would come in our lives and replace us on our own thrones. We all have a little Herod in us, but in the end the question we must answer is how do you replace God? Listen to God respond when man attempts to do this:

*Why do the nations plan rebellion? Why do people make their useless plots? Their kings' revolt, their rulers plot together against the Lord and against the king he chose. Let us free ourselves from their rule," they say; "let us throw off their control." From his throne in heaven the Lord laughs and mocks their feeble plans. Then he warns them in anger and terrifies them with his fury. "On Zion, my sacred hill," he says, "I have installed my king."*

*(Ps 2:1-6 GNB)*

The rightful everlasting King already has an installation date set up on the earth. He will always be attacked. The enemy through earthly influence does not want the eternal kingdom to see its purpose performed and completed. It does not want to see the calling and destiny of God fulfilled for the good of all people; which is His perfect will.

The spirit of antichrist is agitated and will work through whatever way possible to kill the possibility of this kingdom being established in and through anyone.

## TIME FOR A NEW KING

It was God's intended purpose from the beginning for earthly kings to only represent the one true King.

Herod resisted the one true King coming. The enemy always has his representative in place on the earth in order to combat God's purpose for that particular place and time. In fact, there has never been a time where there wasn't opposition to the plan of God on the earth; from the Garden of Eden until now.

To what extent will you go to keep the one true King from coming forth in your life? Will you also cut down any and everything from Him that attempts to bring new and better? People who are insecure do this. People who are secure do not let the latest breaking story worry them. They know that they are where they are supposed to be and can't rightfully be removed. If someone greater comes, they accept it knowing it will be for the better.

Like Herod, if you attempt to rid yourself of Him, you actually kill innocent people. People that are supposed to be affected in a powerful way when you accept Him. They miss out because of your refusal and attempts to ensure He never surfaces in your life. On the other hand, if you have the true King living in you, you will always be sought after for destruction, because you pose a threat to evil and prepare the way for the true King to reign on the throne in the hearts of people on the earth as God had originally planned.

If you fear change, like many people do, and refuse to turn yourself over to His kingship because of the cost involved, you will be stuck living in a mere existence which is a settling and rejection of the greatness of potential you were given by God; to demonstrate your best life for Him, thus sabotaging your own future and fulfillment.

Are you ready for the King of Glory to come in? Who is this King of Glory, you ask? King Jesus.

CHAPTER 3

# ATTEMPTED TAKEOVER

*"He had one left to send, a son, whom he loved. He sent him last of all, saying, 'They will respect my son.'*

*"But the tenants said to one another, 'This is the heir. Come, let's kill him, and the inheritance will be ours. So they took him and killed him, and threw him out of the vineyard.*

*Mark 12:8*

That which was always intended for God has always been under fire to be taken over by man. God created the world and everything in it. He gives it to his creation whom He loves and with it the power to rule and care for it. Man decides he will be his own God and do his own thing in spite of God, even suggesting to himself and others that God does not exist and never has and man has always been in charge of everything.

The fact is that humanity can only attempt to steal what never belonged to them. They can never ever have lasting rightful possession. The earth is the Lord's and the fullness thereof; the world, and they that dwell there (Psalms 24:1). Everything in it belongs to Him.

The story here is about a vain attempt for men to keep for themselves the glory of this world once and for all. A man who planted a garden and left servants to tend it saw his sent delegates who were collectors of what belonged to him, get beat up and killed. In this owner's last desperate effort to retrieve what belonged to him, he sent his son - only to watch him get killed. The idea that one could steal for themselves what only belongs to God is insane. The story refers to these people as thieves and robbers.

Man must accept the fact that God will not share His glory with no one, and He is the only one true owner. Yet man is always seeking glory for himself. Jesus stated this when He said in John 5:44, "How can you believe, which receives honor from each other, and will not seek the honor that comes from God alone?" Man hears and accepts man's testimony here on the earth, but won't believe the testimony of God evidenced by signs and wonders regarding who He has sent and declared to be His true kingdom representative.

Today, man has created their own concept of God through the many religions he has formed. Any religious worship that is the result of man-made formation, rules, and activity; is not from above and illegitimate. Men who follow this way do not work for God, but for themselves and each other. He says further that only those who belong to the kingdom can receive the King and follow what He is saying. "You don't hear because you don't belong to God," He says (John 8:47).

What happened in this story has revealed itself again and again throughout other historical events. For example: Just like the workers in this passage, Herod the king, also fought vehemently against a new king. The religious leaders of Jesus day planned and succeeded in killing Him. The very ones sent to represent him were the very ones trying to get rid of Him. It's the same thing happening today. Jesus has seemed to no longer be welcomed in our churches. He has been programmed out. Our focus is horizontal, not vertical. A lot of our church services are about entertaining each other in His name.

A recent news story tells how a pastor has decided not to preach about Jesus in his church because it makes people feel uncomfortable and he says his responsibility is to fill the pews and pay the church bills, so whatever it takes. How do you have a church if you remove the head of it and the purpose for it?

When Jesus came on the scene, a new kingdom had arrived or should we say the first and foremost of all, arrived on earth to take its rightful place in the hearts of men everywhere. The problem was, that which was entrusted to men for the purpose of advancing God's Kingdom, had now in their minds become theirs. They decided to do with it what was pleasing to them. They did not want to release it to the one it rightfully belonged to.

The religious leaders of Jesus day were so intent on staying in control that they paid the guards to lie, after their eyewitness account of His resurrection (Matthew 28:11-15). They were told to say Jesus disciples stole His body. The religious leaders witnessed firsthand the miracles, signs, and wonders of Jesus. They also witnessed the works done by His disciples along with the testimony of the guards, yet they were unrelenting in their unbelief and attacks.

These prideful, pompous, self-aggrandizing, unspiritual hypocrites were full of envy. They were envious of Jesus ministry. They were jealous of the attention He was receiving, and they didn't like their true impure motives being uncovered by Jesus words and works.

"Then the chief priests and the Pharisees gathered a council and said, "What shall we do? For this Man works many signs. If we let Him alone like this, everyone will believe in Him and the Romans will come and take away both our place and nation." (John 11:47) During Jesus triumphal entry into Jerusalem for the Passover celebration, we find that the Pharisees said to one another, "You can see that this is doing us no good. Look how the whole world has gone after him." (John 12:19)

Later, when they finally captured Jesus and brought Him to Pilate to have him crucified, it was stated that Pilate perceived that it was out of envy that they handed Jesus over (Mark 15:10). He realized there was nothing He did that deserved death, and even after hearing testimony stated, "I find no fault with him." (Luke 23:4)

The Jewish religious leaders really wanted the worship Jesus received from the people. They loved the praise of men more than the praise of God (John 12:43). They wanted control no matter the truth or cost. This drive to be worshipped was behind the exit and condemnation of Lucifer, the fallen angel. This happened in the heavens before time began. He is known as the devil, the enemy of God, and His creation. He was the one driving this activity then and is still behind it today.

Compare this to what John the Baptist said when his disciples told him that the crowds were leaving him to follow Jesus. He said, "He must increase and I must decrease." (John 3:30) John stated that Jesus was the reason why he was sent to do his job. He understood that Jesus could only receive what was rightfully His. This is the attitude of everyone who understands who the true King is.

Religious leaders were never interested in the King and Messiah they were told about and supposedly looked forward to seeing. They were too worried about their own place of leadership. They cared more about being honored. They based their right to refuse Him as King on their traditions and laws, not on the mercy and true intentions of the laws they interpreted. They placed their pride over God's miracles, signs, and truth.

Jesus told them, "You study the Scriptures because you think that in them you will find eternal life. And these very Scriptures speak about me! Yet, you are not willing to come to me in order to have life." (John 5:39)

# TIME FOR A NEW KING

It is amazing the lengths some people will go through to keep power and control. They are so blinded that even if the writing on the wall or the facts, counsel, and reality says otherwise they, like a pit bull dog, will not let go. Anytime we refuse to give glory to the ultimate King, and we see ourselves as the ultimate authority in our servant roles, we are doomed. There are many biblical examples of this.

King Nebuchadnezzar in the book of Daniel was warned that his success as ruler of his kingdom was ultimately allowed by God, in whom he should acknowledge and worship. Nebuchadnezzar did not heed the warning and found himself one day overlooking the empire he had and said, "Look what I have done." Immediately his mind was taken from him, and he was in the wild like a beast for seven years until he would acknowledge the truth of the King of Heaven as the Most High (Daniel 4:29-34).

King Herod Agrippa allowed a crowd to say he was a god and not human after a wonderfully, admired speech and since he received this praise instead of acknowledging the truth, he immediately was struck dead (Acts 12:19-23).

Hearing accounts of scripture in the end times when unbearable trouble and excruciating pain will inflict men, and they still curse and refuse to give praise to God makes me wonder (Revelations 16:9). What is working in us where we resist to yield and submit even in disaster or evident loss? The pride in us obviously sticks and has convinced itself that it is worth it. Let me die in pride is what man says. Wow! This is no doubt a strong spirit of rebellion that is working.

Jesus told the scribes, "You are like your father, the devil. He was a murderer and liar from the beginning and there is no truth in him." (John 8:44-45) He has so blinded the minds of people by his lies that they can't see the truth because there is something deep within their core that doesn't want to receive the truth. For some men to acknowledge truth would mean they would have to relinquish their throne and bow down to the one true King.

1 Corinthians 2:8 tells us that none of the rulers of this world recognized and understood God's wisdom; otherwise, they would not have crucified the Lord of Glory. Basically their plan backfired and instead of removing their perceived threat forever, they actually empowered Him as He defeated death, grave, and the powers of darkness that controlled men on the earth. King Jesus took its authority as a man and rightfully, legally gave it to any man that would follow his foot-

steps. Man can't take His throne, usurp His authority, or overtake His wisdom.

Jesus after His death, burial, and resurrection right before His ascension told His disciples, "All authority and power in heaven and *earth* has been given to me." (Matt 28:18)

He disarmed the rulers and authorities (evil forces of this world), He made a public example showing their powerlessness over Him and His truth. He proved His kingship by allowing them to crucify Him and seeing Him overcome it (Colossians 2:15).

Did Satan think he had a chance to overtake God? Does pride blind us to make us think we can actually stand against the creator of Heaven and Earth and win? A created being going against His creator, the student going against his teacher, and a worldly smart person going against the wisdom of the Ancient of Days is unthinkable. No one could ever defeat the true King with all power as was evidenced by His resurrection. The sooner we come to acknowledge His place and our place, the better off we will be. Anything else is insanity.

Lift up your heads all you gates and open the everlasting doors and the King of glory shall come in (Psalm 24:9).

CHAPTER 4

# MAN AS KING

*And the Lord told him: "Listen to all that the people are saying to you; it is not you they have rejected, but they have rejected me as their king."*

*But the people refused to listen to Samuel. "No!" they said. "We want a king over us. Then we will be like all the other nations, with a king to lead us and to go out before us and fight our battles."*

*The Lord answered, "Listen to them and give them a king."*

*1 Samuel 8:7, 19-20, 22.*

Like the other nations around them, God's chosen people in this Old Testament time wanted a king. Today, people continue to look to man to solve all their problems when we are repeatedly told to trust in God and not man. The very core of scripture gives us a central verse that says, "It is better to trust in the Lord than to put confidence in man." (Ps 118:8)

A fallen creation would prefer to have man to rule over them, and not God. We rather have someone in our fallen likeness, not in His created image and likeness. This I believe is preferable because otherwise, we will have to see ourselves for who we really are and have become and reckon so that we can change. We say, "Show me someone who can relate to me and relate to me where I am at, not at what I was created to be." We have become accustomed to the kingdoms of this world being our only kingdom, and we struggle to visualize functioning as a part of God's elevated kingdom.

They were rejecting the rule of God as king. They were making a calculated choice because when we choose a king like ourselves, and God is claiming you recognize Him as your only king, you have determined who you will serve. Upon your decision, you rid the other one claiming to be your king by a process of elimination.

Many struggle to walk with the true King because they never remove the threat of the man-made king in their life. They are under the idea that they can both coexist together without one affecting the other. Darkness and light; evil and good; good fruit and bad fruit; none of these work together to attain the God planned destination. Jesus said you can't serve God and wealth because you will ultimately hate one and be loyal to the other. You can't serve two masters (Matthew 6:24). How can two walk together unless they be agreed? (Amos 3:3)

Samuel, the current prophet and judge of Israel in this passage of scripture, is displeased with the Israelites request brought to him of granting them a king to rule over them. God knows he is dealing with a stubborn, rebellious group of people from the days of bringing their forefathers out of Egypt. They were humans, like us, who were prone to always wandering away and looking to themselves or elsewhere for their salvation and fulfillment.

Samuel warns them that God said if He grants their request, they will be sorry. Under another man's kingship, they will lose themselves and children to a life of servitude. Their best service, work, strength, and harvest will be required for the man-made king's pleasure. They will work for the king's purposes and not their own, nor for who they were created to serve. How about you? Do you work for the government of man or the government of God? God continues, that when they cry out against the unjust actions of their chosen government, He will not hear because it was what they asked for.

The people said, "We want it anyway." They would only be satisfied when their form of government was like all the other nations who did not serve the Most High God. They wanted man to decide for them and to fight for them. How do you conclude to have another man represent you when God has been the one responsible for saving you from all your past enemies? They are now asking to be oppressed by their own people. They now want to look to man who couldn't save them as their main hope.

Even with this, there were still men in the kingdom who disregarded and dishonored His new pick. They did not like God's selection, and they insulted Him. Nothing has changed, for even today people will continue to pick who they want, and they want God to pick who they want. They will not be happy with anything but what they deem to be right. No men will always agree with each other so there will always be the threat of a coup or faction party in earthly governments. The real reason people strive says James 4:2-3, is because they don't look to God and they don't receive His answers because their motives are wrong. They are looking out for themselves only.

I see governments around the world today calling for current officials and leaders to step down because they are untrustworthy. The people of those countries can almost be guaranteed that those political groups who want to be in power instead, will rule no better. The promises they make is to be put in power, so they can take care of themselves and those who helped them win. The majority of them really could care less about what happens to everyone else.

People like to point the finger and expose the faults of their fellow elected kings. The heart of the man you desire to replace is evil, they say. However, this is the same type of heart they usually have. They are just deceived to believe they are righteous and can do better.

My wife and I always taught our children as they were growing up that there are only two kind s of people in the world; those with the heart of God and those without. Unless a man fears God and has surrendered his life completely to Him, how can he expect not to sin and be overcome by the wickedness all around him on his own.

Israel's loyalty was not to God, not to others, but really to themselves. I believe even now, through bribes and lies, many representatives in government are props so that a minority group can get and have what they really want. I would dare say that we have puppets running most of the government positions in many countries today.

The religious Jewish leaders, that had a form of godliness but denied the true power, chose where their loyalty was. It was with themselves. Caesar and Pilate allowed them to be in power regarding their own people. They represented their people to Roman officials. And people were afraid of them. They had the power to excommunicate people from the church, arrest, imprison, etc. Their religion was full of rules - dry, dead, and powerless to change anybody or anything.

This sounds like many churches and professing Christians today. You can always tell those leaders who are not really walking under the rule of the true King of Heaven. They make a big deal about being honored. They see themselves incorrectly. They don't understand that to be great; you must be the servant of all. They do things to be seen. They crave exposure for themselves. Their focus is on material things. They are full of pride and envy and only desire honorable positions. While there are men serving in their church who may have no shoes, they will not lift not one finger to help someone else but insist they follow the law of God. If they do anything good, it's only because they have ulterior motives.

They, like the false leaders of Bible days, condemn others for their sins without mercy and without considering the cause.

The people had become the servants of humans. They put themselves in the hands of mortal men. Their hope, help, and salvation would rest on one like themselves. How scary? When one can't save them, only then will they look for another alternative. This is allowed by God. Man has to be allowed the freedom to make this choice. Like Israel, he won't see his sinfulness any other way. Man, however, continues to try to find one like themselves only to keep getting the same results. It is only when God picks His righteous representative, such as a David, Solomon, and finally King Jesus – our Lord and Savior - that peace and prosperity for all is experienced.

It has always amazed me of how man is but a vapor - a breath away from being gone, yet so boastful about their life and enamored with themselves and abilities. We are so great at looking good outwardly and covering our weaknesses without admitting how dysfunctional we are inwardly. We are great at defending ourselves with excuses that keep us from accepting the truth.

## CHOOSING BARABBAS

Pilate, not wanting to see Jesus crucified, tried to release Him based on the practice of prisoner clemency given to the Jews once a year. The people could release Jesus the King or Barabbas the murderer. The notorious Barabbas had been arrested and jailed for committing a murder among his community. Despite his guilt, the people were encouraged by their religious leaders to ask for him instead of Jesus.

When you ask for a man to be your king, instead of Jesus, you are asking for a Barabbas. When you reject King Jesus as your Lord and Savior, you have asked for the spirit of death to be released in your midst. Through a mortal man comes sin and death, only through the man Jesus comes forgiveness and life.

They exchanged truth for deception and chose guilt in the place of innocence. 1 John 5:12 says, "He that has the son has life and he that does not have the son does not have life." So if you reject the son, you reject life, and the result is spiritual death, physical death, and eternal separation. Physical death is only temporary, but you are also refusing the light which leaves you in darkness forever. In Him was life and that life was the light of men (John 1:6).

Barabbas is someone like yourself who doesn't pose a threat to your heart allegiance. The nation of Israel would kill an innocent man, like the murderer they asked for killed an innocent man. They did this in the name of religion. They did this so they no longer had to be challenged with words like repent or you must be born again. They wouldn't have to change their ways for a different king if we just keep one like us. Barabbas represents mankind; he does what we do. When they released Barabbas, they were releasing a murderer like themselves. Only Jesus can save us from ourselves.

During the time of Jesus, the Jewish nation, which had a rich heritage with an awesome history and culture, were known as Israel, the people of the one true God who would produce the Messiah and restore Israel making it an everlasting kingdom of rule. Yet they forgot and mentioned none of this and saw themselves as subjects of another man, Caesar. They would look to anyone else as their king, as long as it was not Jesus.

When the crowd was presented with the statement by Pilate, "Shall I crucify Jesus, king of the Jews? They responded that they had no king except Caesar. No doubt, Caesar was the king of Rome. They readily accepted the earthly king but rejected the King of kings. He was the very one who gave Caesar his throne. The man Caesar would be judged by Him one day. Yet, he was of the Earth, something they could see and control. Jesus was a king with a kingdom that was beyond earth; something man could not control.

The issue will always be, "Who is in control?" Man or God, You or Him. We accept man as king because we want to be in charge. When we accept God as king we allow Him to be Lord. When He is Lord, we do not do our own thing; we surrender to do His thing. If we call ourselves His representatives and don't obey His commandments, then we deceive ourselves, and His response to us is, "Why do you call me your Lord and do not do the things I say?" (Luke 6:46)

## CHAPTER 5

# WHAT IS TRUTH?

*So Pilate said to Him, "Then you are a King? Jesus answered, "You say that I am a King. This is why I was born, and for this I have come into the world, to testify to the truth. Everyone who is of the truth listens to my voice." Pilate said to Him,*

*"What is truth?"*

*John 18:37-38*

And Pilate wrote a title, and put it above the cross. And the writing was, JESUS OF NAZERETH, THE KING OF THE JEWS (John 19:19). God, through his sovereign hand, ensured that this would be the written testimony that all would read as our Lord and Savior was atoning for the sins of the world to establish himself as King for all time.

Pilate declared this truth even though we are not sure whether he believed it or not. Perhaps it was the conclusion Pilate came to as a result of hearing the testimony of Jesus himself. Whether he realized it or not, he prophetically wrote the correct title on the sign placed above Jesus.

Many of the Jews read this title as it was placed where Jesus was crucified near to the city, and it was written in Hebrew, Greek, and Latin. Those who were responsible for plotting His death complained to Pilate about this title that was given to Him and written for all to see.

He was the King of the Jews, whether accepted by the people or not. The truth must be told and never changed. I have written what I have written is what Pilate said. Like Pilate's refusal, we must refuse to change the truth no matter who likes it or not. It would be the title all would see and all who saw it would have to decide whether they would accept this claim.

Of course, the Jewish religious leaders rejected this as a possibility despite the miracles, testimonies, events, power, wisdom, and authority they witnessed. They were intent on putting Him out of sight and out of everyone's mind so they could continue to do unproductive church business as usual.

In their request for a title change, they said make it say His claim. For in their mind His claim was the problem. It was what made Him guilty. He considered Himself equal to God. He calls Himself a King, the Christ, Messiah, and Savior. He said He was the creator of life when He actually was a mere man they concluded.

In their eyes, Jesus was a troublemaker; breaking laws and perverting the truth. They said He was subverting the nation when He was actually speaking the truth and challenging the lies and hypocrisy. Their sins were being exposed. Their dead system of works was being revealed.

Pilate marveled that Jesus did not defend Himself against them. When he asked Jesus if He was a king, Jesus told him to consider what he had heard and make a decision on whether he believed it or not. After Pilate heard Him, He was sent to Herod, a Galilean in a different jurisdiction. This Herod was glad to hear Him. He always wanted to see Jesus in action, and here was his chance. However, Jesus was not a performer and neither would He respond to the false accusations. Herod after examination found no fault in Him as well. After being sent back to Pilate, Pilate decided to chastise Him and release Him because no one saw a cause of death except those who plotted to kill Him.

In Pilate's attempt to release Him, he was being threatened by the Jewish leaders of changing his allegiance from King Caesar. Anyone who releases a man who claims to be a king is challenging King Caesar and is not a friend but an enemy of his, they said. Although this was not really the case, the Jewish leaders would make that case. They would then no doubt plan to appeal to Caesar.

Pilate's relationship with his subjects was important to his position as governor. The discontented Jewish leaders would work to make it possible for Pilate to lose his own throne with this lie or by being seen as one not capable of ruling his own region well.

This was consistent with one of the tricks that the Jewish leaders tried to use against Jesus. If they could prove that Jesus was dishonoring Caesar the king, they would have no problem ridding themselves of Him. They had tried it by sending a hired false witness to ask Him in a crowd whether it was good to pay taxes to Caesar. Jesus knew their evil scheme and never forbade tribute to Caesar; instead answering, "Give to Caesar what belongs to Caesar and give to God what belongs to God." (Matthew 22:21)

Jesus could do this because as a legitimate king of His own kingdom which had always existed and knowing all other kingdoms exist by Him, He being above all, He was never threatened and afraid of another king in any other kingdom. He knew He was not fighting for the kingdom Caesar ruled. Jesus said, "My kingdom is not of this world." (John 18:36) His Kingdom was not limited to a place or specific people. His Kingdom is established and built in the heart of men everywhere.

Pilate saw the scheme and knew the intentions of these chief leaders. He was now caught in a dilemma. He thought, "What should I do?" In the end, the voices and cries of the Jewish leaders and their followers prevailed along with his fears. Pilate gave in to them and delivered Jesus to their will.

Pilate found no fault or wrong in Him, but he allowed Him to be crucified. He wasn't behind it, yet it couldn't happen without him. God was not shocked by Pilate's decision. He was a pawn in His plan to help carry it out by His foreknowledge. Eventually, with or without Pilate, the sacrifice takes place, but woe to the one who helps. This is similar to Judas who played the part of the traitor.

The Bible says Pilate knew the real reason why Jesus was hated by those who plotted against Him;

ENVY. His wife even had a dream about Him being a righteous man. Jesus never needed to defend Himself. In Jesus words, Pilate had heard the ring of truth. He tried to save Jesus by offering Barabbas, scourging Him and talking to the crowd, but when he could do nothing else; he washed his hands and turned Him over to their requests. He still had some responsibility. He was offended because the cost was too high.

Maybe you are like Pilate, and you know something because there are too many things pointing toward the truth of who Jesus really is. You have a tough decision because your own throne would be at risk. Like Pilate, to side with Jesus would offend your own authorities. You are saying to yourself, "I can't afford to lose my seat." You may be framed as a traitor by your own friends and family. Their tumult would put your seemingly secure position in this life at risk. The only way to save your seat is to cooperate, do what they ask and go against your better judgment. You try to find a way to stay in your seat and clear your guilty conscience. The real issue is you don't want to give up control of your life to gain it in Him. He is the absolute Truth.

How do we go on when we know the truth of the matter deep inside? How do we just try to ignore and avoid the subject? We then avoid people who may remind us what we really know as truth. Will we continue living with the battle inside until the last day where admittance is unavoidable? The King you must then face and declare who He is. For every knee will bow and every tongue will confess that Jesus is Lord to the glory of God the Father (Philippians 2:10-11).

How much will it cost you? When counting up the cost, you may find that you have no trust in God; only in the authority He gave you. Would you rather sit in a place of honor on earth for a short time than to sit in a place of honor in heaven with the true King for eternity? What choices are you making? Do these choices benefit you in the long haul? Do you have more faith in what was given to you, your free will, than in the one who created you with it?

The goal of the evil enemy is to stay in power – to be the main influence at all costs. He will work hard to shut down any real perceived threats of truth to his kingdom of lies. The enemy has come to murder the Truth. Jesus said, "I am the Truth." (John 14:6) Satan did everything he could to kill the Truth, but he couldn't. The spirit of truth can never die, and the man who is the Truth overcame death. The Truth lives on.

Satan is still willing to do whatever he can to deceive people. He does this illegally and deceptively behind the scenes but must make it look legal to the public. Everyone must believe that something is wrong with the Truth and not them. As many as possible must come onboard in condemning Jesus for the best results. We can see the secular media doing this today.

We see how at all costs our major institutions of learning, do everything in their power to remove Christ material, silence believers and support immorality, teach only evolution, and promote gender confusion to our youth. I look at the eyes of our youth today, and they are crying out for real answers. They are internally dying from superficial, unsatisfying teachings, activities, and material things they are constantly being fed. They may seem temporarily happy on the outside at times, but they are void of the real joy they should always have.

Most news today is so slanted and negative, I refuse to watch or read it. When I was growing up, it used to be that everyone was innocent until proven guilty. Today, that is only in words; many are treated guilty by all upon media coverage; before they even have the chance to enter a courtroom. Many use their power to influence how they want you to think before you ever really know the true facts behind the story.

The crowd of unbelievers, during Jesus day, quickly joined in with the evil leadership. It is amazing to me how everyone just followed along with the word of evil, religious leaders. Before our very eyes, we are reading how the chief priests are persuading the people to ask for a murderer to be released instead of the only one who could save them all.

Today, representatives of the apostate church are leading flocks astray as they turn the gospel of our Lord Jesus Christ into a license to sin and a for-profit business. They persuade people to kill the real Jesus of the Bible and create one that is more accepting and inviting, up to date, and works with secular humanism in our current world.

However, just like in the days of Elijah, God has reserved thousands that have not bowed their head to another king. Are you one of them?

## CHAPTER 6

# WISE MEN

*When they saw the star, they rejoiced exceedingly with great joy. And after entering the house, they saw the Child with Mary His mother; and they fell down and worshiped Him.*

*Matthew 2:10*

Everywhere you find a king; you will find a company of wise men. There has never been a kingdom that has had a king without a chosen group of men serving him as his advisors. They function in different roles and take on many responsibilities. These wise men are studied and learned men put in place to assist him in running his kingdom. They handle the affairs of the kingdom answering to him and following his will. They have given their lives to studying, learning, growing, and leading others.

Wise men are those who are seeking to understand everything imaginable. They give major time and thought to life's events, its meaning, and how everything fits together. Wise men are looking for the truth and its application. These men were consulted for their skill and abilities in interpreting signs and symbols. Like astrologers they were to be experts of the times and seasons, have knowledge of signs, dreams, visions, and prophecies as they were important in helping to determine world matters. These men had to be bright and sharp.

Several people in the scripture functioned in the role of wise men. Daniel and Joseph stand out among the many. In Daniel's role as chief advisor, he had to come up one day with the dream and interpretation of the king he served; this saved him and his friends' lives. Joseph was also a trusted, wise advisor to his master and ultimately his dream interpretations and advice to the Pharaoh landed him the country's governor's job. Daniel and Joseph handled the affairs of the major kingdoms known as Persia and Egypt.

The scripture gives us great details on the preparation process of wise men as well. In Daniel chapter 1 we are told that King Nebuchadnezzar instructed the master of his advisors to bring some of the children of Israel, who met the qualifications for serving, into his administration. They had to be young men, good looking, gifted in wisdom, possessing knowledge, and quick to understand. These men had to have the aptitude for learning the kingdom's language and literature. We are told four Israelites, (Daniel, Hannaiah, Mishael, and Azariah), stood out.

Our true King also has a kingdom where He has wise men who are seekers of truth. These are men who meet the King's standards, seeking and acknowledging truth while sharing this truth with others. They are men that worship unashamedly because they understand their place. They understand the scripture that says, "If you seek me you shall find me when you search for me with your whole heart." (Jeremiah 29:13) They are glad to be in their position. They recognize their greatest benefit is that they have close access to the King. Their role is not to sit on the throne, but to serve the King who sits on the throne. They await their call from Him and work for Him with passion and excitement.

Wise men seek after God with a voracious appetite. It is seen in their pursuit. They are not so engaged in distractions. They follow the true King at the expense of all worldly knowledge. In their estimation, all Godly knowledge always supersedes any other knowledge. The Apostle Paul of the scripture counted all his worldly knowledge as dung compared to the knowledge he gained in his relationship as a servant of the Most High. I believe one of the greatest challenges today to accepting Jesus as King is worldly wisdom. This world's knowledge alone doesn't fix the root of man's continual problems. God's thoughts and ways are higher than men, yet the wisdom of God is foolishness to this world.

These particular wise men were coming to find the location of the promised King with the intention of worshiping Him. Wise men seek the true King and when they find Him, they take on a role of worship and service. Unwise men seek to remove Him, instead of serving the King's purpose. Wise men still seek Him after all these years.

Many may read this book and say I already seek God and know Him. However, you may really not. Going to church and saying the sinner's prayer is not the same thing as knowing Him. How do you separate one who really knows Him from another? This is a great question. I think you have to ask yourself some hard questions and answer them all honestly.

Is God first in your life? Is prayer a priority? Is fellowship with other believers a priority? Does the scripture have the last word in your affairs? Does your lifestyle, conversation, finances, and time reflect His Kingdom or this worlds? If you were accused of being a born again believer and disciple of Jesus Christ, would there be enough witnesses and evidence to convict you?

Why is it as people who say we are saved and represent the Kingdom of God, we see little progression and minimum results? Our growth seems to be stunted, our knowledge is limited, and our impact invisible. If the only time we pray, read our Bible, or talk about God is when we attend church; there is a problem.

Most companies are aware of when it is time to make changes for the better. They are always looking to improve and be on the cutting edge. They move in this direction no matter how great they think they are already. Yet in the church, we believe we have arrived. We seem to stay limited in our mind. We come to church to do the same old thing. We don't expect anything greater. We come with prejudgments and assumptions. We can't receive more because we don't expect anything more. We await others to do something we haven't seen and to stir us to a new excitement. We are led by our feelings and emotions and look to gratify our sensual desires. We focus on the external - looking good - and abdicate disciplines that solidify our internal spiritual condition. Scripture says, "These type of people praise me with their lips while their hearts are far from me." (Matthew 15:8)

We get bored with God because we don't spend quality time with Him and we don't truly believe in Him or know Him. God is fresh and alive, and His mercies are new every morning, and His faithfulness to us is great. Oh we believe what we heard about Him, but not to the point of experiencing this for ourselves. The cost to pay to really know Him, we don't value Him enough to pay that cost. If He makes it easy for us, that's what we are looking for; Gain without pain; Growth without sacrifice; and progress without change.

Let me ask you a question. What kind of commitment did it take for you to become a professional in your line of work? What kind of dedication did you have to give to become a nurse, lawyer, or a captain in the army? It is amazing to me the hurdles we are willing to jump over to accomplish our goal in this life, but the excuses we make as to why it's fine to be half-hearted in our efforts as workers in the kingdom of God.

The wise men were studied men. The star represented the Savior. They understood the times and realized what was going on. The problem with God's people is they think they know God. They think they have

Him figured out. The spirit of God told me one day, "My people are operating on limited knowledge and resources. They are lazy when it comes to knowing me." They enjoy themselves, gifts, callings, while their relationship with me is purely based on a social network." The Lord told me, "My people are destroyed because of a lack of knowledge." (Hosea 4:6) This knowledge is first-hand intimacy with God that comes only from a most sacred relationship.

God wants to know: Who is He to us when there are no other church people around? His so-called people love the thought or idea of being a Christian and what comes along with that, but Him and all that He is does not really appeal to those who are driven by natural appetite and desires. In His love, He has attempted to strip them of their idolatry and allow them to experience frustration and trouble, but they just see it as a need to get over until they return to where He does not want them. God is actually trying to get us to a better and safer place that we can't see. What we already know - was good to start, but what we need for today and the days ahead that God desires to share with us, is found only in His secret place.

God says, Turn your hearts to me completely for I am sending latter rain on the earth to cleanse it from impurities and restore it back to God consciousness. Repentance is a gift and is needed. Recompense your ways to return to your first love and to buy from Him bread that will satisfy and fountains that spring forth. Do not live dead, but die living. Rescue my people who are hurting. Rescue them from the pit that has been set and the trap that has been made. The goal of the enemy is for them to believe I don't care and I don't exist and for them to live dependent on their own ways, but I am calling you away because I will smite everything that is not according to my way, plan, and purpose.

Wise men will heed this call. He that hath ears let him hear what the spirit of the Lord is saying to his church (Revelations 2:29).

CHAPTER 7

# RELIGION VS KINGDOM

*You search the scriptures; for in them you think you have eternal life: they testify of me. And you will not come to me so you might have life.*

John 5:39

So there is a man from Puerto Rico who claims he is Jesus. There is another man in Australia that claims he is the Christ and his woman's name is Mary Magdalene. No really, I'm not making this up. I'm sure many people have made these claims since the time of our true risen Savior, Lord, and King. I think what causes my eyes to widen and mouth to open in amazement is the number of people they were able to convince and the following they have.

I remember my crazy uncle during a family dispute telling our whole family that he himself was God. I will never forget it. When he said the words "I am God," I thought he would be struck down any minute. Even though I was just a boy, I knew better than to believe he was God. He was crazy and capable of doing and saying some wild things I give him that, but creating us, being holy, or performing miracles was a laughable thought. It was scary because you could tell he actually believed it.

He had always been the king of his life, most of it in prison under a warden. Yes, it's sad because I guess he was god in jail regularly for his stubborn, rebellious nature. He was not afraid to get in the face of anyone; he would say and do whatever he felt he wanted to and when he wanted. In his mind, there was nothing anyone could do about it.

It was much later during a visit to my home as an older man that he shared his life story with me. I listened with utter shock and surprise as he shared the abandonment he faced as a child and the rejection of his own parents who had given up on him and his wayward ways. Their tough love had turned into being unloved to him, and this was the root of his pain which continued to be expressed through defiance to everyone especially God.

It didn't help that his parents were ministers. How could parents, better yet parents who were ministers give up on their child? A prevailing thought indeed, but they were human, not perfect and definitely not God. God will never leave you nor forsake you regardless of who you are and what you have done. He is a God of second chances for all who want to come to Him.

I also had a family member who has passed away. He was at peace in his last years since he had turned his life around. During his last days on this earth, he was always sharing the good news of Jesus with others. In one conversation with me, he had shared how his ruthless life had affected others and got him booted out of his church organization of which his family had been a part of many years. He could not attend any family weddings or funerals at the church as well.

After he had got his life together, he went through the process of reinstatement and was still turned away. He struggled with the idea of how could God and his representatives turn their back on people who were truly sorry and wanted a second chance. I remember telling him that you can't always associate God with those who claim to represent Him.

Kingdom representatives don't always represent the King appropriately. Some don't represent him at all. Some are liars. However, we must remember they are not the King or possibly a part of His Kingdom, and you can't let them become a distraction. One consistent thing that I come across regularly in life is hearing the many stories of hurt and pain as a result of the church. The stories are never-ending. I too have many experiences and could fill a book sharing my own disappointment and frustration with the church institutions.

One guy shared a story of how he went to a church, heard the gospel message and went to receive the Lord in his life, but when he came up to the altar, the speaker told him he wasn't really ready yet and wouldn't let him give his life to God. Could you imagine this? Oh, my God! How could you judge someone's heart? This is between them and God. This is a mistake you wouldn't want to make and have someone's blood on your hand. This kept this man from making Christ his king for many more years, but he eventually overcame the experience to accept Christ as King without allowing another person to get in his way.

People all over the world have legitimate experiences (not excuses) of being derailed and pushed away from God through their life episodes with so-called

Christians, men of the cloth, and religious organizations. There is too much to name that has happened under the banner of church and religion…such as incest, child molestation, pride, abuse of power, sexual misconduct, and financial abuse. Everything you see happening in our world at secular places can also be found in our religious structures. People are fed up with the hypocrisy and unaccountability of those who say they represent the true King and his Kingdom.

I get it. You expect it or can understand it with the secular world, but with the church world who is to be separated as people living with a higher standard as an example to everyone else, it is a shame. From the beginning, God has wanted to operate as supreme King to a chosen people on the earth, yet they have found a way to keep the name He has given them while rejecting His true kingship and misrepresenting who He really is.

Look at his chosen people Israel whom He says about them that His name is blasphemed among the Gentile nations because of their betrayal and behavior. (Romans 2:24) There will always be those that say they are and do not or are not.

We are all familiar with the Roman Catholic Church in the name of God and the publicity of the abuse on innocent children over many years. I'm of

Pentecostal upbringing, and though I am proud of my spiritual heritage, I am not blind to the fact that several of those in leadership, and others who have promoted great Christian music have been exposed for financial irresponsibility and immoral failures as well.

However, none of this negates who the true King is and His power. In our secular world if someone is caught misrepresenting his company or organization they may be dismissed. In the Christian world, many seem to get away; however God is the ultimate judge, and His judgements are righteous and perfect in timing. Everyone must be judged individually and according to his own works. This means you won't be judged according to what someone else does or doesn't do; only what you do regarding the truth you know. Truth doesn't change because someone else doesn't apply it or they apply it wrong.

When you look at the cross and at the King, what are you going to do about that? This is where our eyes must be. He was still the King of the Jews even when the same Jews were killing him in the public arena. The so called religious structure did their best to give him a black eye back then. There were prejudice Jewish converts (Acts 6:1). There were so-called Christians using the Bible as a tool for slavery, and religious zealots in the name of Christ killing innocent people throughout world history. I mean whatever your hang-up is with people don't let it be with God and the worship of the one true King. Don't let it be your reason for missing out on a relationship with the King and entering His eternal kingdom.

Religions created by man is for the purpose of those men alone. Religion is man-made by them for them, and God's kingdom is God made by Him for you. You are His reason for building and preaching the Kingdom. Don't ever forget that.

## CHAPTER 8

# KING AND WEALTH

*No one can serve two masters; for either he will hate the one and love the other, or he will be devoted to the one and despise the other. You cannot serve God and mammon [money, possessions, fame, status or whatever is valued more than the Lord]*

*Matthew 6:24*

Judas was one of the twelve personally selected disciples by Christ Himself. He was a follower of Jesus during His earthly ministry. The twelve chosen followers were named apostles (sent ones) who were sent out to testify concerning the Kingdom of God which had now come. King Jesus, their master teacher, would prepare them so upon His exit they would continue with His power to fulfill the great commission.

The biblical account about Judas lets us know he was given the duty of care for the offerings that were given to Jesus ministry as he ministered (John 13:29). Judas job duty would be referred to as treasurer in today's world. It is important to note that Judas heard Jesus teachings firsthand. He saw his miracles up close. He was a member of the original Jesus team. He went out when sent and reported back to his Master teacher with the rest, being excited about how demons were subject to them. Everything seems to be looking good, but we actually have a betrayer in the midst who will carry out a deal to hand Jesus over to His enemies.

From the beginning of this story, who would have thought a different character would be revealed emerging. He had the name of being a disciple, but he was different from the rest. Judas reminds us that what is in you will inevitably come out of you. Some fruit trees look alike at first until you see the fruit growing on it. Jesus says a bad tree at the root can't bear good fruit and a good tree at the root can't bear bad fruit (Luke 6:43). You will know them by their fruit; trees or people.

Upon fruit checking Judas, the initial idea that perhaps the tree is not what we think, isn't quite detectable. In the twelfth chapter of John, he is bothered by the fact a woman pours out expensive perfume oil on Jesus. Look at his response, "This should have been sold for the poor." Wow, now isn't that the heart of a good man. He definitely appears to have the heart of God from this statement. He seems to care very much about the poor. Anyone observing this from the natural would commend him on what a compassionate heart he has. We may deceive ourselves and easily fool others, but God knows the truth and what was now covered would soon be revealed for what it truly was.

The scripture tells us that his reason for saying this was not his care for the poor. He really could care less for the poor. Here is a character trait of many who even claim to follow our Lord Jesus Christ. They do things in the name of God and our Savior that appear righteous outwardly, but they are filled inwardly with wrong motives. They are building their own kingdom using the name of the one true King. They, like Judas, are called followers. They look the part and act the part but are really hypocrites – actors who play a role.

It was revealed to us by the writer that Judas real reason of anger and dissent regarding what he believed should have been used for a greater cause was about him. He was the great cause. His desire was to have more money to steal out of the bag, which he apparently did regularly. He was a thief in hiding. He was stealing right out from under Jesus ministry, and Jesus knew it but didn't say anything. That's right God will allow you to hang yourself eventually in time. There was no need for him to deal with Judas. Judas work had to be completed, and he would trap himself, he would suffer himself from his own decisions.

Think about this; Judas walked with THE TRUTH, yet was never convicted. Many people may believe that God must be fine with their unrighteous behavior because he doesn't seem to say anything or nothing happens short term from their unrighteous practices. God is merciful. He is constantly speaking and teaching. The word is all around you being taken in, but is there any change? How could you be around Jesus convicting words and not feel any sorrow for the deception you are practicing? There was no space in his life or heart for this King Jesus because his heart was already worshiping another king, RICHES. Remember you can never serve two kings at one time. You must decide. You must give up one to serve another.

The point is that there will always be people who pretend to be ready for a new king to come into their life. They are professional actors driven by greed and unrighteousness motives and worldly riches. They embrace Him outwardly with open arms, but their real agenda is themselves. What is in it for me? Will I gain power, prestige, glory, control, material possessions, or fame?

We are reminded to continually check our hearts. Life's happenings and our responses to trials and temptations come to reveal what is in us. Like the expensive perfume being poured out was used as well by God to reveal or bring out what was really going on inside Judas. Where your treasure is that is where your heart really is (Matthew 6:21).

In fact, if we are following Judas storyline, we see what he does after he gets a non-agreeing response from the Savior regarding his concern. By watching his actions, we learn a lot about the character of those who have another agenda than the group they are supposedly serving with.

He immediately goes out to speak with another group; in this case, the religious leaders, enemies of Jesus. He went and sought out Jesus enemies to see how he could get compensated for helping them in their plan to capture Jesus. His heart is revealed. He wanted money, and this was an opportunity. People who love and worship money are greedy. They are always looking for an opportunity to gain more. It becomes an addiction. They have a never-ending appetite that is not easily met.

Jesus response to Judas was to leave the lady alone who poured out the expensive oil. He also stated that her worship was costly, real, and would always be remembered as God was using this for His glory. In this, Jesus showed He wasn't as concerned about the money in the bag as He was to the service and worship that flowed from the heart.

Maybe Judas thought of Jesus as a crusader, a new King that captured the attention and hearts of people. He then figured if I get in on the ground floor, I could be in a great position once this thing takes off or blows up. Those not willing to submit truthfully to the King will always operate with a carnal mindset. He probably thought, if we end up leading a kingdom and overthrowing the Romans, I'll have a seat of authority. Think about how much money that will be coming in that I'll then have access to and I will be set. The fact that Jesus could give all of the money away and not care must have really bothered him.

Judas was not interested in the Kingdom of Heaven or allegiance to this new King. It was only about how this King was going to help him get what he really wanted - more money. Once he saw that this might not happen, what loyalty is there? I'm loyal to you as long as I'm getting what I want. Have you ever known someone like this? Maybe this is you. Maybe being a follower of Jesus is a means to your desired end, not His. What are you really in this for? Your true motives will be found out because like one who undresses, God has a way in life of stripping off everything to expose what is really underneath.

Maybe like Judas, once you see a more advantageous opportunity, you will be jumping on the other side. Saying I'm out of here and basically, how much can I get as a traitor? We have preachers preaching every Sunday while subconsciously asking their audience, "How much will you give me as a traitor?" How much if I don't preach against sin? How much if I let you do whatever you want and never hold you accountable for your actions? How much for tickling your ears, compromising the truth, and making you feel good? If I help you with your agenda in exchange for God's, how much will I get out of it? This is shameful, but this is real and going on constantly. It is time for real relationship with the King.

There is also another warning for us hidden in the pages of Judas life. Many of Jesus sermon topics were connected to money and Judas being a follower no doubt heard these parables and admonitions. Yet he never dealt with this issue in his life. He surrendered to its temptation countless times until it finally cost him his very life. What we refuse to deal with after being warned time and again by God will very well decide our destiny - how and where we end up. What part of your life have you not submitted to the King? How many different times and ways has God tried to lovingly correct you, but you won't have it?

Jesus is saying to us that refusing to obey Him will be very costly. If your right hand offends you, cut it off; it is better to lose one part and live, than to go whole into everlasting punishment (Matthew 5:30). What are you allowing in your life? What are you justifying when God is dealing with you to let it go? You can't serve the King of kings and be the king yourself. Whoever you obey that is who you serve.

God is not mocked. He is not a fool, and don't you be one. Whatever you sow, you will reap. Don't deceive yourself; stop saying you are under King Jesus when you live against the principles of His Kingdom. Just admit you are your own king and haven't made up your mind to embrace the true King yet.

## RICH YOUNG RULER

There is a story in scripture (Matthew 19:16-22) about a rich young ruler who comes to Jesus, referring to Him as good. Jesus always responds to people that the only one who is good is God. I would always read this wondering why Jesus would respond this way. I finally understand that Jesus was challenging people to see if they were acknowledging Him as one who came from God or as an ordinary man. Thus the thought process, if you say that I am good – Are you saying that you recognize that I came from God? – If you are saying that you recognize I am from God, then will you put your faith totally in me?

The rich young ruler wanted to know what commandment he needed to follow to enter into the kingdom of God. Jesus response was not typical. He knew that all the commandments can be fulfilled by obeying the first two: Love the Lord God with all your heart, soul, and mind; Love your neighbor as yourself. However, Jesus doesn't mention either one, but instead starts naming the other commandments that follow such as: Thou shalt not steal; Thou shalt not commit adultery; and so on.

The young rich man felt relieved that he had never (to his knowledge) broken any one of these since his birth. So Jesus tells him, if you want to keep the commandments perfectly you must sell all you have, give the money to the poor, and you will have your riches in heaven, and live the rest of your life down here in self-denial following me in doing kingdom work.

The young rich man hung his head in sorrow. He was grieved at Jesus response because he had a lot of possessions. It seems the more one gathers, the more one becomes accustomed and attached to his stuff; it becomes very hard to let it go. Jesus knew this, and that is why He mentioned the commandments He did. He knew those specific commandments were not an issue for this man, but the main issue was his love for his riches. This is rather seen in the first and greatest command which is to Love God with everything, over everything, and above everything. The young man instead loved his riches above God, and that is why he walked away sad when he was given the choice between the two.

It is also worth mentioning that when the young man asked Jesus his question, Jesus looked at him with great love. I believe this is mentioned for us to see that the love King Jesus had for him was not the same love he had for Jesus. I can feel Jesus eyes beholding him and saying, "You don't love me like I love you."

Also in the passage found in Mark chapter 10 relating the same story, Jesus told the young rich man that he was lacking one thing. God revealed to him what he lacked. He was missing an uncompromising love. When the King comes; He comes to rule totally. That means He is coming for everything. There must be nothing in the way. There must be total rule.

He is requiring total allegiance because He is above all. He is the author of life, so He has the right. You are rightfully His creation. Secondly, because true fulfillment and joy comes from Him foremost. Everything else and everyone else will hurt, disappoint, fail, or leave you still unsatisfied in your soul (being), but He will not and never will. He is dependable.

It is hard for a man who trusts in his own riches to enter into the kingdom, but God is able to help you see what is really important if you want. What seems impossible to man is possible with God. Remember money flies away like the wind. It is not true wealth. Don't let the riches of this world deceive you and make you miss out on the true riches that His followers will experience forever. Don't let money be your king.

## CHAPTER 9

# KINGDOM RULES

*Do you not know that the unrighteous shall not inherit the kingdom of God? Be not deceived; neither fornicators, idolaters, adulterers, effeminate, abusers with man.*

*1 Corinthians 6:9*

Anytime there is a new king; there is also a new way of doing things. In regards to the King and Kingdom of God vs the kingdom of this world; the difference is like night and day. Our way versus His way. He says His thoughts are not like ours and his ways are not like ours, as the heavens are higher than the earth so are his ways higher than ours and his thoughts higher than our thoughts (Isaiah 55:8-9). When you give way to a new king, you should expect changes. If you are not willing to change you are not ready for the new King.

I have been blessed to travel throughout the world. I am aware of the fact that each new country I travel to brings not only its unique culture but also its own set of laws that one must abide by to function there. I must submit to the authority in that place if I want to take part in it. The Kingdom of God is a place of its own and has rules. How do we expect to play by our rules in His Kingdom, and expect the new King to accept them? This doesn't happen, but some are deceived into believing that it does.

When you have lived so long in another kingdom, you have to get used to a new way of doing things when you leave for another one. At first, nothing seems to make sense because everything is so foreign. As I look at other countries I may ask, "Why is the steering wheel on the other side?" Why are cows allowed to roam in the streets while I'm trying to drive?

Change is not easy. Change is not readily welcomed. Change is uncomfortable. It is like getting rid of old habits and forming new ones. Years ago, I worked as a dispatcher for an asphalt plant. Within the year that I started this job, it was bought by an oil company. One of the immediate changes that was made was the operating system we used for all our paperwork. I had become accustomed to the way things were done and begrudgingly learned the new one, thinking there really was nothing wrong with the old one and if it's not broke why fix it.

After time went on, I began to appreciate only over time the new system seeing the greater benefit and need. It was built not just for what we were doing but for where we were going as a company. It was much more efficient. No change for companies means falling behind and eventually falling out of the race altogether. Not making the necessary changes spiritually when the time has come will also threaten your life. You must take the time and make the adjustments needed.

Operating in a new kingdom under a new king is different. The king sets the standards; he makes all the laws the citizens must abide by in order for the kingdom to work and represent who he is and what the kingdom is all about. The Kingdom of our Lord and Savior Jesus Christ exemplifies this. Let's look at some important elements of how this Kingdom operates.

# LOVE

His Kingdom is about love. God loved the world so much that He gave His son. His son loves whatever the Father loves and submitted to His plan of giving up His life for mankind. The new commandment, the son, King Jesus, gave to all his servants was to love each other. This would follow the example of this royal family, God the Father and Jesus Christ, the son. Everything is done with love and by love. Nothing is done by force. Love looks out for another to the point of making sacrifices to meet another's needs. The Kingdom of God is filled with love, and everyone is expected to operate according to this love.

This love means that everyone in the Kingdom has been forgiven of their misdeeds and must also forgive others of their faults. They must forgive in the same manner that they were forgiven. No one with un-forgiveness can be a part of the Kingdom of God.

The greatest trap for many would-be followers is the offense done by another that people refuse to forgive. Un- forgiveness will keep you from being accepted by the new King (Matthew 6:15). You can't accept the King while rejecting your brother. Look at what the Bible tells us:

> *If anyone says, "I love God," and should hate his brother, he is a liar.*
> *(1 John 4:20).*

> *Whoever loves his brother remains in the light and does not stumble, whoever hates his brother walks in darkness.*
> *(1 John 2:10-11)*

> *If your brother sins against you, be willing to forgive him seventy seven times*
> *(Matthew 18:21-22).*

> *First be reconciled to your brother, and then come and offer your gift*
> *(Matthew 5:24)*

These and many other scriptures make clear to us that God will not forgive you without obedience to this command and that accepting the true King requires one to make right his relationship with others. God is not joking on this matter. This one thing will literally keep you out of the presence of the King and His heavenly Kingdom. Forgiveness is serious business. Please don't ignore God's warning. Get it right with whoever you need to.

We must also love the King above all things. We must love the Kingdom more than we love our mother, father, sister, and brother (Matthew 10:37). We must love the King above anyone else. He must be first. He warns His church before His return in Revelations to return to their first love, or they are in danger of being removed altogether.

I was listening to a wonderful song by Jonathan McReynolds one day entitled *Make Room*. What caught my attention was the initial lyrics,

> *"I find space for what I treasure.*
> *I make time for what I want.*
> *I choose my priorities*
> *Jesus, you're my number one."*

If you want to know where someone's heart is don't listen to what they say, just find out how they spend their time and money, and that will tell you everything you need to know. God is serious about us not having any other gods before Him.

I believe this generation's biggest idol is carried from place to place in their hand: a cell phone. I used

## TIME FOR A NEW KING

to think that TV, video games, sports, and recreational drugs were addicting; but I think that handheld phone beats them all.

Loving him above all includes our family, culture, and country. We have been given wonderful examples in scripture of those who truly loved their King, and willingly sacrificed everything for their relationship, and were rewarded.

In the book of Daniel, we have the story of the King's top administrator. He was targeted because of his position and spirit of excellence. Some of those under him wanted him gone, so they plotted to destroy him. They knew that the only opportunity was to make him choose between his God and his life. Without his knowledge, they approached the king with an edict requiring all to honor him with no one praying to any other god for a particular time or else they would be thrown in the lion's den. The king signed it with his signet ring, meaning it could not be revoked. Daniel prayed to his God three times a day as always despite the edict. Expecting this, the plotters found him and reported it back to the king for the execution. The king loved Daniel but couldn't save him from the edict. God protected Daniel in the lion's den. Daniel showed that his love for his God will never be compromised by any law that would separate him from his God.

The story of the three Hebrew boys during this time also shows us the dedication one must have. They were told to bow to a statue, and they refused to obey the king's orders. They were thrown into a fiery furnace, and God protected them. They and their God received recognition throughout the kingdom. Like these, we must learn to take a stand for our King and truly believe what we say we do.

The disciples of Jesus, Peter and James, refused to obey the religious leaders of their day. They were told not to speak about Jesus. They were beaten and threatened. Their response was that they must obey God rather than men and chose to continually obey their call with greater boldness and accept whatever consequences that may come. We must never honor people above God.

We are told a king of Israel named Saul disobeyed God because he feared people. God calls everyone in His kingdom to be led by Him and not follow the ways of man when they are in opposition to His commands. Sometimes you have to be unpopular and all by yourself. Your faith has to be greater than your feelings and strong enough to conquer your fears. Kingdom citizens should always honor and respect kings from other kingdoms, without giving up allegiance to their own king.

## RIGHTEOUSNESS

The Kingdom is righteous. Everyone in the Kingdom must be in right standing with God. This means you accept the King on his terms, not yours. We must first acknowledge we are sinful apart from God and need a Savior. Many who claim Christianity have missed this concept. They are convinced they are good, moral people without God. They believe they have good hearts naturally. In order to accept the King, He must be the Truth. The truth from Him is that we are all filthy, born in sin and shaped in iniquity, none of us are righteous not one, and all our righteous deeds are as filthy rags to Him. We need to be reborn spiritually, washed, cleaned up, and made righteous by Him to be able to stand before Him.

We must acknowledge we are dirty, let Him clean us up by recognizing and accepting his sacrificial death where His blood was poured out to atone for our sins. It is the only thing that can remove sins and make us not guilty and blameless before the King. There is nothing else that makes us worthy to be accepted. Neither is there salvation in any other for there is no other name given under heaven by which man must be saved (Acts 4:12). Jesus is the only one that allows us to stand blameless before the Father. In His kingdom, you must be righteous, in right standing before God, standing in his righteousness (perfection) and never attempting to stand in your good works, because our works will never be good enough.

Accepting Jesus birth, life, death, and resurrection is my only hope. If I believe this with all my heart and confess this with my mouth, I am saved (Romans 10:9-10). True belief and confession are seen in my actions afterward, and my follow through to the very end. God has completed His part, and upon receiving Him our new spirits are complete in Him as well, but our outer man starts at this point being conformed to His image until the end of our life journey. At the end of our journey on the earth, we will receive the full hope of our salvation. During our lifetime, if we stay attached to the King, then we are good; if we get unattached then we are in trouble.

> *If ye know that he is righteous, ye know that every one that does righteousness is born of him.*
>
> 1 John 2:29

## HOLY

The King and his Kingdom is Holy. This means He is totally perfect and without any spot, wrong, or darkness. He is without defect and spotless in every way, thought, and idea. This Supreme Being is fully virtuous and pure; therefore, nothing with any deficiency can stand in His presence without grace, mercy, and His covering. Yet He commands everyone in His Kingdom to be as He is. "Be ye holy, for I am holy (1 Peter 1:16)." He expects holiness. He does not wink at or excuse blatant sin or hidden sin. Sin, missing God's set standard, is serious business. Remember it required a high price to be dealt with; suffering and bloodshed to be exact on our behalf. Yet many who say they follow this King, practice behavior that is unholy; not only those who do it but also those who support it and are entertained by it, are guilty of grieving the Holy Spirit.

In Galatians chapter 5, we are given examples of behaviors practiced that can cause us not to enter His Kingdom. These behaviors include adultery, fornication, idolatry, wrath, strife, murder, drunkenness, and so on. There are no exceptions. Living a holy life is a requirement if King Jesus is to be your king. There is no compromise, no treaty or agreement. His law is law.

You have His mercy that triumphs over law, but doesn't excuse heartless devotion and intentional sinning.

His Kingdom is not a democracy, there is no voting, no majority rule, no appeals, no disobedience, and rebellion allowed, and no excuses accepted. The way is indeed narrow, and the King doesn't apologize for it. There is no need since He is the creator of everything. This is the way He wants it.

## JUSTICE

His Kingdom is just. God is a God of Justice. He is fair. His scales when weighing are balanced. He judges without partiality, holding each man responsible and accountable for what he knows and what he has been given. You are always required to do what you know. A man who knows to do right and doesn't do it is in sin. It is righteous judgement with merciful consideration since He also is a God of mercy. Time is always given, warnings are as well.

The scripture is very clear that man must give an account for every deed done in the body. He will give an account for every word he spoke as well. If we have asked forgiveness, our sins will be covered.

He must appear before the great white throne of judgement to receive any rewards since he surrendered his life to the King on earth. All must appear before the Judge at the court of Heaven. The prayers and cries of those who seemingly got away with murder on earth will not evade heaven's court. All will be avenged from innocent bloodshed on the earth, and every wrong will be made right and dealt with. His servants will serve as judges one day in His heavenly Kingdom if they are found faithful. This will happen when the kingdoms of this world become the kingdoms of our God.

One of my favorite parables Jesus tells is in the book of Luke chapter 18 about a widow and a judge. This story is told to Jesus followers to teach the importance of diligently praying with faith. The widow was wronged and sought justice and was denied it by this earthly judge that had no fear of God. The widow in her daily persistence of coming and crying out to the judge for justice showed she refused to be denied what was rightly hers.

Jesus said it was her persistence that caused her to be victorious. He then adds that as a righteous judge, will He not avenge his elect that call out to him without stopping. Don't give up on God because it appears evil has won out. It's a trick of the enemy to make you believe it doesn't pay to be righteous and choose King Jesus. He will try to convince you that God is not just. That He doesn't exist and if He did He is cruel because of all that has happened to you in life outside your control.

The thing about kingship is you have to trust Him and know who He is; when you really know who someone is, you can vow for them even if you don't understand what is happening to you. The story of Job and Joseph are great examples of not understanding how seemingly unnecessary hardships fulfill God's plan and works out for your good in the end. You have to give a person a try to see if they are trustworthy; to see if they can fulfill their promises. You have to give the King a chance, stick with Him long enough to see the benefits of his Kingdom. In the end you won't be sorry. He says, "Come unto me all ye that labor and are heavy laden and I will give you rest. Take my yoke upon you and learn of me for I am gentle and lowly of heart and you will find rest unto your souls (Matthew 11:28-29)."

In conclusion, the Kingdom of God is righteousness, peace, and joy in the Holy Ghost. It is totally controlled by the Spirit of God. Where the spirit of the Lord is, there is liberty (2 Corinthians 3:17). This means freedom from the bondage of sin and freedom to enjoy the true peace, love, and joy that comes only from the King and from being in His presence. It can never be taken away. It can begin here on earth in the midst of a fallen world and continue without disturbance upon our exit from here forever. Heaven must be a wonderful place.

## KING AND THE WEDDING BANQUET

The Kingdom of Heaven we learn in Mark chapter 10 is like a king that prepares a wedding banquet for his son. He sends out invitations through his servants to tell his guests to come, they refuse. A little later, he sends them out again to ask them to come because everything is now ready. They refused again heading off to do their own earthly affairs and duties; and worst, others instead abused the servants who were inviting them, killing some.

The angry king responded by sending some of his army and destroying the murderers and their city. He then says, it is time for the feast, but those who were invited were not worthy to come, go find others on streets and bring them in and fill the house. So all were gathered from all around, bad and good, to fill the place.

When the king comes to see all the guest who had come, he spotted a man without the proper attire. This man who was invited into the feast by the king into his kingdom obviously came in doing his own thing. He decided to wear his own clothes instead of the clean garments provided for the guests.

This man couldn't answer when asked by the King, "How did you get in here without your wedding garment?" He was then thrown out to a terrible place. This story is told to let us know the importance of meeting the King's requirement. It comes with a required dress code once in. He didn't get away and neither will anyone else. The garment is given by the King to wear. It represents His righteousness covering our filth. Jesus ends by saying many are called, but few are chosen. God invites everyone to be a part of His Kingdom, but only those who come and change are chosen to actually eat with Him. We must allow God to change us.

I remember listening to a man who shared a dream. He shared how he was practicing sexual immorality and one night while sleeping; he saw a man who he believes was Jesus. This Savior came to him and embraced him with a hug. This man said he felt a love like no other at this moment. After showing this man so much love, Jesus then walked to a table and invited the man to join Him in fellowship, but told him he had to first give up the behavior he was practicing. As the man stood there, looking at the Lord, he said it was as if the Lord could read his mind of his unwillingness to renounce this sin. He then said the Lord told him he had to go he could not remain there with Him.

People must realize God is holy and for Him to allow anything contrary to what He is would make Him no longer who He is. Real Love doesn't let you do whatever you want, especially when it knows it will destroy you. Real love wants to save you, even from yourself. God's love does what is best for you. God's plan is to give you a hope and future (Jeremiah 29:11).

The story of the King and his wedding banquet details to us how God was rejected by His own people, Israel. This gave an opportunity for the Gentiles (non-Israelites) to be offered salvation. Like those who were invited and refused to come, maybe that is you. Maybe like them, you made light of His invitation. You may have dishonored and disregarded joining the King in His Kingdom.

Perhaps you were like the man who had enough faith to come, but not enough to change. He came with the wrong motives. He saw it as not a big deal and unnecessary. He thought he could come as he was and he could, but didn't understand he couldn't stay as he was. He did not take advantage of the clothes provided. He was a spectator more than a participator, but that was not possible here. He did not expect the king to notice, but everyone knows you never come into the presence of royalty any kind of way. You must always present yourself before a king as a person worthy to enjoy his kingdom.

Here is a very important point: once he was seen by the king, he had no more chance. He was now judged. Just like on earth before we die, we have the opportunity to do what is right. We can choose the right way and follow the right king. After this life is over and we appear before the King who is also Judge, it is too late to change. Our decision is finalized based on our last current state before our transition.

I'm afraid, so many will find themselves on the outside of the Kingdom because they were unprepared and believed a lie. The King Himself has stated the rules, and we can't believe someone else who is not connected or representing Him wrongly. We have the Holy Word of God given by God to guide us. There is too much at stake for us not to get our information from the source itself and verify what is necessary to be a citizen of the Kingdom of Heaven.

King Jesus has come. He came to His own, and His own did not receive Him, but to as many that did receive Him, He gave the right to become the children of God even to them that believed on His name (John 1:12). It is time to give up everything for the new King, time to remove ourselves from our own throne. Time to get it right this time, once and for all. Time to realize this is the perfect time.

# CHAPTER 10
# KING OF HEARTS

*Lord, wilt thou at this time restore again the kingdom to Israel? And he said unto them, it is not for you to know the times or the seasons, which the Father hath put in his hands by his own power.*

*Acts 1:6, 7*

Like many of us today, Jesus followers were concerned about what was going to happen to them, their family, and their country. At their present time, the Roman Empire was in power and had taken control of their area. The people had to pay taxes to the Roman King Caesar. They were under the rule of those he put in power over their region. They were not a free state but wanted to be free. They desired to independently control their own affairs. The disciples wanted to know when they would become their own rulers.

Maybe surprising to many, Jesus was not concerned about this the least bit. He seemed to discourage His followers from taken up worldly causes and rather give their attention to causes that have eternal implications. These were of the greatest importance, and everything was to follow this lead. For example, in taking care of the poor, He said, "You will always have the poor with you." (Matt 26:11) Nevertheless, He still took out time to assist the poor, but the goal was so that they might believe in Him whom God has sent. His purpose was that the poor be rich for eternity, not just for the moment. What good would it do them to be given riches in this life and upon death descend to an impoverished state forever? Everything done was to point people to eternity. After all what does it profit for a man to gain this whole world and lose his soul (Mark 8:36). There are many people who have attained fortunes in this life, but died and left it all, leaving here spiritually impoverished. What good did that wealth do them in the end?

So many projects I have personally been a part of; from building schools, providing college scholarships and educational services, providing needed transportation, building bathrooms, etc. All these projects helped people, but let's put things into perspective:

If I am helping build wells so people can have water, this is a great cause. Some no longer have to spend the whole day trying to get it because it's many miles away. They are better able to survive; they experience less disease, can wash, cook, and bathe. Clean water is a necessity for life. A village is undoubtedly benefitting from this water. Now, a few years later, a catastrophic disaster causes all to die, and they are now suffering in eternity with no water because I never offered and provided them the water that will make sure they will never thirst again.

I'm talking about an introduction into an eternal kingdom where they have access to a King who provides all things with abundant supply on Earth as well as in Heaven. This is the best scenario.

Amazing the passion of conviction I see with people regarding so many issues, from religion to politics to sports to social injustices. People are affected by many different happenings and live their life and spend their money to try to correct or proselytize others to see things their way. When you try to compare the concerns of these earthly causes in light of the eternal gospel, you are referred to as not empathetic to the cause and therefore heartless. You can be marked as unrealistic and being so heavenly minded that you are no earthly good.

It is not that you make light or minimize the atrocities of life, but you understand everything must be put in its perfect place and time. There will NEVER be peace on earth as long as humanity is in charge. There will always be racist. There will always be corrupt government. There will always be religious hypocrisy and worldwide injustice in this life. This doesn't mean we don't fight, but rather we should understand the fight.

No matter how hard we fight the injustices of our day, everything and everybody isn't going to change. I do believe the fight is worth the group that will be reached, but not in exchange for their souls. We know that there will always be a remnant of people who we can help to change their mind, but how will the ultimate seed and fruitfulness of change truly happen? It will happen by a change of the heart. There is no cause that has been initiated by man that is able to change the human heart. It can persuade the mind and thoughts but not change the heart.

Herein is the reason for Christ seemingly noninterest in the political matters of His day. He understood that the problem for Israel was not their sovereignty but their character. Their heart was the real change agent that could eliminate their problem. The change in their physical position would only reveal it. So many look at the problems in the world from the outside, not realizing the problem is from within. The reason there is dictatorship, control, inequity in power, serfs and peasants, the have and have nots is because of the condition of the human heart. There is enough food and money in the world for everyone to be fed and be made well, but when evil hearts rule - the people cry (Proverbs 29:2).

If the time came for you to rule without the heart and spirit of an all-good God controlling your life, the same problems would occur. The issue is not: Who is the king of the country, but whose heart does the king have? Who is the king of the individual hearts in His kingdom? Without the true King in the heart, man operates selfishly only looking out for his own interests.

Israel, God's chosen nation, had failed many times to represent their God and His ways to others. Israel needed to first experience salvation from within in order to operate it from without and so far, they had refused to see their spiritually impoverished condition. We know Israel will one day be fully restored. This will happen in the very last days of earth before the final world war called the Battle of Armageddon. At this time, all the enemies of God operating against His chosen people will be destroyed for good as the almighty King of kings comes to their aid.

Jesus is doing with His disciples, whose mindset is to make Israel a great earthly kingdom, the same thing with us today; taking our eyes off of what we think we bring to the picture and placing it on what only He can bring. Their kingdom was to demonstrate His Kingdom. Their king was to reflect the King; it's useless otherwise. Unless the Lord is building the house, all the labor will be in vain (Psalm 127:1).

How can they do this if they are not familiar with the Kingdom they are supposed to reflect? Hence the reason Christ came to them and the reason for His response here. Once the disciples understood that His Kingdom is seen in the life of those who wholeheartedly follow Him, then their focus changed, and their proclamation of the Good News was settled. They would now all await the hope of the Kingdom that will never be shaken, the one promised by God that will endure forever instead of their own temporary, earthly one.

Do we understand? Are we still asking God to restore something on earth that will never fix the real problem? Are we working with symptoms? Are we aware of the root issue? I remember hearing a story about a village that was trying to save babies who were seen drowning in the river. They were encouraging as many to come and help as there were not a few. However one man stopped and ran away after helping for a while, and others followed him, and when they asked them where he was going, he said to stop those who were putting the babies in the water in the first place. Sometimes we expend so much energy helping the hurting instead of fixing the root that started the problem in the first place.

I've learned it takes harder work to fix a broken pipe than to replace it. Many people don't want to put in the discipline to fix the problem at the outset. They rather put the emphasis on stopping the bleeding after it starts. One is reactionary, and the other is precautionary. God never deals with problems by looking at ongoing symptoms. His goal is a total fix and a permanent solution. He says, "Who the Son has set free is free indeed." (John 8:36) He knows true freedom starts with getting to the real issue, the root or core of the matter.

It reminds me of how a plant will always grow back after you cut it down unless you uproot it. Weeds will return again and again unless they are destroyed at the root. We must take away what is causing the destruction in the first place.

Rome wasn't the main problem for Israel. This may be a hard question for some, but you must ask yourself "What is really causing my problem? Is it the rich? White people? Minorities? Politicians? Being unlucky? The devil? Family? Are you overly concerned with what other people are doing? I believe if we knew as much about God and invested in His cause the way we buy into all these other campaigns (Me Too, Black Lives Matters, etc.) we would be powerful enough to make the necessary changes in our lives and truly help others.

When will there be peace? When will blacks be treated equal? When will all women be treated equal? When will the poor stop being exploited? I can answer that question. It will happen in the Kingdom of God. In the meantime, help as many people turn their hearts to God so they can experience it firsthand otherwise your greatest physical effort will have minimal results because only God can change the heart – the real problem.

The disciples became focused on heart change and on the message that changes hearts. The Kingdom of God is here. We have heard and seen the Lord. He is the King of all kings, and all that accept Him will be a part of a Kingdom of peace that will rule all kingdoms forever.

The Kingdom and King is about the change of the heart. This is why Jesus told His disciples let the times and seasons happen. He knew the changes of God had already been planned out. In the meantime, receive my power and be my witnesses all over the world.

There is only one power that can defeat or overcome every societal ill, and it is not in the world or of the world, so no movement from or founded in the world that is not from God himself will or can overcome its problem. The idea that it can is a deception and a smokescreen. It instead becomes part of the problem because it hinders man from getting to the real answer. It is man's answer to man's problem. Man thinks he can fix it himself; therefore, it becomes a never-ending issue. The problem is a spiritual one, and the effects of sin can't be defeated by human means. A supernatural dimension is needed and has been made available by God himself.

In concluding this chapter, when I look at everything in light of eternity, where should my priorities be? You may say I'm too preoccupied with Heaven and Hell. I would respond that your statement is an excuse to reflect from the truth. We have life insurance, car insurance, dental, medical, and retirement. Why? Because we know we may eventually need it and never know when we will need it. This is not overly concerned; this is just being smart. Preparation is wisdom applied. We do this because we know how our life may be affected adversely without it. We want to have the proper care for ourselves and our families. Yet many choose to ignore the fact that we really have very little say or almost no control of when we will take our last breath. Despite this knowledge, some still choose to take no course of action for their eternal security.

I believe this kind of thinking is unwise. Our pride and sin's grip on us will cause us not to ask ourselves the most important question, "How will we spend eternity?" Contrary to others beliefs, we don't get to decide to cease to exist after this life or come back as something else.

Only what you do in this life with King Jesus will last. As servants and priests of His, we are to do what He will have us to do. Just like He does, we must get to the root of the issues and focus on what's truly important. We must seek and operate according to our King's perspective.

CHAPTER 11

# KINGDOM INVASION

*The devil taketh him up on a high mountain, and showed him all the kingdoms of the world; and said unto him, all this power will I give thee, and the glory of them: for it has been delivered unto me; and to whomsoever I will I give it. If thou wilt fall down and worship me, all shall be thine. Then said Jesus to him, "Get behind me, Satan: for it is written, that we should worship the Lord God, and serve him only.*

*Luke 4:6-8*

How was Satan able to offer Christ the kingdoms of the world? How did Satan get all the kingdoms of the world? He said it was given to him. Who gave Satan rulership over the kingdoms of the world? Man did. Satan proposed a deal and man took it when in the Garden of Eden he chose to obey him instead of God.

We are offered the same deal today; we just don't realize it is Satan who is behind the proposal. He offers power, wealth, stardom, freedom, etc. He has it dressed up in pro-choice rights, LGBT causes, media influence, secular humanistic books, technological advances, scientology, social media, man-made religion, etc. Maybe you took the bait and were deceived. The promise seems to get you everything you want down here, minus your soul.

God's kingdom was the first and will be the last in Heaven and Earth. The kingdom on earth was given to man. The kingdom of darkness, created through rebellion, could not exist in Heaven once its leader and participants rebelled. It had nowhere to operate. It was a kingdom without any land; just spirits banished to the earth realm with no authority to function; roaming through the air.

It seized its opportunity when God created man and placed him as ruler over the earth. Therefore, this created earth that belonged to God was given to the man He created to rule it. The kingdom of darkness attacked the Kingdom of God through man on the earth and stole influence and possession of it through trickery. This kingdom of darkness, operating the same way today, has taken possession of the nations of this world.

## OVERCOMING DECEPTION

The tool of deception and trickery was the only way Satan, ruler of the kingdom of darkness, was able to get it. In order to defeat this evil king and kingdom, you must be one step ahead of it, and since God knows all before it takes place, He had a plan. It is crucial we hear from God by continually seeking Him, if we intend not to succumb to this rival and defeat Him in the end.

God spoke to man from the beginning as well as every prophet He selected. He had his spoken words written down for us. Lastly, He spoke through His son Jesus who came to the earth. Jesus said, "My sheep hear my voice and another one they will not follow." (John 10:3-5) It is critical we listen and obey the voice of the King.

World History is filled with examples of transfer of land by trickery and deception in order to gain unfairly what somebody else wanted. For example: the United States government did this in taking land away from Native Americans. Trickery was sometimes used instead of straight-up war to reduce casualty and the possibility of loss. The Bible also records stories of deception by one group to gain dominance over another or protect themselves from another. Some historians believe that Israel was tricked out of their possessions in Goshen by the Egyptian Pharaoh after Joseph's generation died. This led to Israel becoming slaves after having been so prosperous in the land.

Jacob was continually tricked by his shrewd uncle Laban. Laban became rich off of Jacob's labor. Wherever there is deception, you can trust that the enemy is always involved. This is who he is and what he is known for. All forms of lying can be traced back to him. The scripture says he was a liar from the beginning and the Father (source) of all lies (John 8:44).

Satan, the enemy of our souls, tricked the first woman Eve, who fed the first man Adam, who didn't refuse to eat what God told him not to eat. They got kicked out of the Garden of Eden because of this act of rebellion while Satan, the prince of darkness, gained man's kingdom through this rebellion. Rebellion is always followed by loss. Since that time, there has been a universal battle.

Just like he did with Eve, Satan works overtime planting thoughts that go against God and his word. His goal is to make God's truth look like a lie and make his lie look like the truth. Whatever you submit to, you serve. Whatever you obey, you serve. Whatever you yield to, that becomes your Master. Satan wanted and tried to become Jesus master like he had become Adam's master.

In Matthew 4:4 He tempts Jesus in the wilderness even telling him to bow down and worship him for an exchange of all the kingdoms of the world. Jesus was not falling for it. He came to fix the problem, not compromise and lose this most important battle for mankind's salvation.

## VIOLENCE

We have a fight on our hands. The world is evil, corrupt, and under the control of the evil one, and under his power. It is a fight between the only two kingdoms there truly is; all other earthly kingdoms will fall into one of these eternal spiritual places.

## TIME FOR A NEW KING

We have the Kingdom of Heaven in its attempt to save man with the truth of the gospel delivered by God's earthly servants since the days of John the Baptist. On the other side, we have the kingdom of darkness, who from the beginning has used violence to try to overtake God and stop righteousness on earth. We are told about a war in heaven between Michael, the archangel of God, and Satan and his angels. Satan and his angels lost and were kicked out of Heaven for good.

After winning his right to influence on earth through the first fallen man Adam, he continues his violent war against those who follow God. This is seen with a wicked Cain, who killed his brother Abel because his own actions were evil and his brother's righteous. Through wickedness and violence on earth, floodwaters are sent by God to start again with a righteous man, called Noah. Attack after attack against God's people from the edict to murder them during the days of Egyptian slavery to the days of Queen Esther to days of Jesus, where Herod ordered the slaughter of baby boys in hope of ridding himself of King Jesus. There is the killing of the prophets and of His disciples. And of course the bloody crucifixion of Jesus. Today the violent onslaught continues through abortion, gang homicides, suicides, abuse, and sex slave trafficking among others. This is all the work of the devil.

The Kingdom of Heaven had not appeared on the scene until John the Baptist, who paved the way for Jesus. King Jesus arrival could now allow everyone access to the Kingdom since His reason was to destroy the works of the devil. The devil brought into the world works to produce sin which brought death. King Jesus of the Kingdom of Heaven accomplished something greater than this by coming as a man to the earth to suffer and die for sins and being raised from the dead, taking all power and the authority of death, hell, and the grave.

Violence ensues now even more because the devil is mad that his power has been stripped, and the only way he can get and keep control over people is through deception. He fights to keep others from knowing this truth, to keep them away from God, to keep the gospel away, to kill, destroy, and steal anyway possible. He works to keep people ignorant of the truth, tempting them to reject God. He uses the deceitfulness of the riches of this world, lust of the eyes, lust of the flesh, and the pride of life.

People are still coming to the Kingdom despite his attacks. It is, however, forceful men that lay hold to it.

Those that push past the crowd and the opposing deception, entering into the truth. It is a battle. The crowds came eagerly to hear John, who preached a baptism of repentance and told the crowds to prepare to believe in the one who will baptize you with the Holy Ghost. John wanted to get men clean so God could pour into them what He had planned. However all men didn't want this, only those who were bold enough to be ostracized by others entered.

King Jesus comes on the scene to bring as many to God that would believe in Him, but many have chosen not to follow. Many religious leaders of His day were the main hindrances. Jesus called theses leaders, "children of the devil." They consistently combated Jesus words and ministry.

Today this attack against the true Kingdom is seen, even under the guise of religious orders. The enemy's main goal is to stop the true church, the light of the world. So one of the best ways to stop it is to become a part of it and turn it from within and make it something it was never intended to be. The prince of this world is clever in his plan to draw many away from God and toward himself. The real church is in the way of him being in total control of this world. Our prayers hinder his work from being done. He has no power over the real church.

God's Kingdom is the object of unbelievable hostility, but the plans of hell shall not prevail against those who are truly a part of it (Matthew 16:18). Christ true followers have been left on earth as the King's heavenly ambassadors to bring about His Kingdom.

## BATTLE

As we face the opposing force, we must realize this is not a physical fight. Our Kingdom is much more; it is not of this world but another. If we are going to win and lay hold or come into the Kingdom, we must be aware of how to overcome the forces against us. We must be empowered and completely plugged into the greatest and highest source in our Kingdom, King Jesus.

We are told to put on the whole armor of God so that we can stand against the tricks of the devil. Our battle is not against flesh and blood, but principalities, powers, rulers of darkness, and spiritual wickedness in high places (Ephesians 6:11-12). We must understand we are dealing with spirit beings and physical weapons won't work. Our most powerful weapon is figuratively described as a sword. It is the words of our Savior and

King. A king's word has authority to accomplish anything he needs to do in his kingdom. King Jesus is no different. If we have been given permission to speak on his behalf, then anything we say according to His will has to be done (1 John 5:14). It is automatic. His word reigns supreme in any land where He is the ultimate authority, and the earth is included.

2 Corinthians 10:3-5 says we walk in the flesh, but do not war after the flesh; for the weapons of our warfare are not carnal (physical), but mighty through God even to the pulling down of strongholds, casting down imaginations and every high thing that exalts itself against the knowledge of God, and bringing into captivity every thought to the obedience of Christ. As national teacher and author Joyce Meyer says, "The battlefield is in the mind." I attest to this and believe whichever king controls the mind, controls the person.

Furthermore, you can't expect to be in a battle or win a war without some sacrifice. There is always a price to pay. The enemies of darkness would come after Jesus, who willingly was crucified for our sins and rose again to secure our victory. They would kill disciples Paul, Steven, and many early church fathers even in the name of God.

Today they will attempt to silence believers with lies, jail, persecution, humiliation, evil reports, and murder. People in countries all over the world are risking persecution and death to advance the gospel. The scripture encourages us by stating, 'They overcame the enemy by the blood of the lamb and the word of their testimony and they did not love their lives unto the death." (Revelations 12:11) Are you willing to sacrifice your life? Trust me when I say the Kingdom of God is well worth it. Any temporary afflictions on the earth we experience can't compare to the glory that awaits us for all eternity (2 Corinthians 4:17).

In Jesus name, I pray everyone reading this book would come into the Kingdom, if they haven't already. Come and rule with the everlasting King. To be in this Kingdom, you can't be weak. It takes guts, everything you have, all your devotion, energy, purpose, and determination. It will take your commitment, time, mind, work, and plan to be freed, remain free, and free others from this dark, evil, wicked, corrupt generation and its ruler.

## CHAPTER 12

# IT'S TIME

*Jesus said, "The men of Nineveh shall rise in judgement with this generation and shall condemn it: because they repented at the preaching of Jonas and behold a greater than Jonas is here."*

*Matthew 12:41*

The city of Nineveh, a non-Hebrew town, received a warning from a foreign Hebrew named Jonah. He came to visit their country and declare the judgement that will happen to it very soon because of its wickedness. The reluctant Jonah had been entrusted with this message from God. In the story, we find that the message obviously cut to their hearts and made them think. They knew the ugliness they had been involved in, and it took an angry, mad prophet to come and make them face it. The words caused conviction to the most important person in the country, the king.

In the king's mind, there was only one solution. We will repent, fast, and plead for mercy, and perhaps God will change his plan of judgement. The decision was decisive, and his words were spread to all his subjects in the country. God heard their cries, He saw their actions, and they were saved from potential disaster. God showed as always that He is loving, compassionate, and merciful. He is not willing that any should perish, but for all to come to repentance and be saved (2 Peter 3:9).

Why did they fear the God of Jonah and His message? I believe that Nineveh, like other surrounding nations, knew about the history of the Hebrews and their God. They were probably familiar with the prophets before Jonah, such as Jeremiah and his accurate predictions regarding Babylon destroying Judah. They thought, what would the result be of not heeding this message? Are we willing to take that chance?

How about you? What do you do when you hear the King's warning of impending judgement? Is it a joke to you? Are you not afraid? The king of those people repented in sorrow and asked the King of all kings, the God of creation, for one more chance.

This story of Nineveh is found in the book of Jonah. Yes, so you see Jonah is not just about a man swallowed by a fish as much as it is about the mercy of God on sinners. God is looking to spare and save mankind despite their wickedness. He wants them to be saved, and He is looking for every opportunity He can to show His love and mercy to them.

It shows us the very heart of God; that His message of judgement was a tool used to get them to repent and turn to Him. It is a warning. God warns us over and over again. What a great and merciful God we serve. He does not want anyone to perish in their sins.

The witness people had during the time of Jesus was much more than Nineveh had, yet they did not repent. Our witness is even greater today, so what is our excuse? We are left with none.

During King Solomon's reign, the Queen of Sheba recognized his wisdom that came from God. We now have the King of kings and His words. How shall we escape God's righteous judgement if we neglect such a great salvation? (Hebrews 2:3)

This salvation is near you; even in your mouth, and in your heart; that is, the word of faith, which we preach; that if you would confess with your mouth the

Lord Jesus and believe in your heart that God has raised him from the dead, you shall be saved (Romans 10:8-9).

For everyone that calls upon the name of the Lord shall be saved (Romans 10:13). God has also provided us with the Holy Spirit sent from Heaven to dwell within in us so that we will be sealed until the end. We are given power by Him to do everything Jesus has asked of us.

What else do we need? What are we waiting for? How many warnings do we need? How many messages does it take to make the decision we need to?

He that hath an ear to hear, let him hear (Matthew 11:15). Jesus is saying, the issue is that everyone can hear, but not everyone is interested in listening. What kind of ear do you have? What kind of appetite do you have? What are you looking for? Are you looking for truth? Those who have an ear for truth, hear what He is saying and those who don't, won't hear what He is saying.

The consummation of time is upon us. God will separate the wicked from the righteous. Just like there are only two kingdoms, the Kingdom of God and the kingdom of darkness, there will only be two groups of people and two destinations. We have the righteous and the ungodly. We also have Heaven and Hell.

Jesus says He will separate the sheep from the goat. He will separate the tares from the wheat; the good tree from the bad tree. The one will be burned and will fall condemned and judged at the end, while the other will rest at peace and experience a Kingdom that will never end.

There are two things we can be sure of about God and his timing in doing everything he has planned when it comes to final judgment: God always warns mankind and God's judgements and wrath are never poured out on his righteous servants, but only on the wicked. Let's look at some examples of this in scripture.

➢ Noah found favor with God when God wanted to destroy all men off the face of the earth. God instructed Noah to build an Ark of safety for him and his family. God gave man 120 years to hear His message and repent. (Genesis chapter 6)

➢ Abraham was promised Canaan land as a possession by God to his descendants, but it would be four hundred years later after the sin of the Amorites had become full, and God's destruction of them would be justified. (Genesis 15:16)

➢ Abraham's nephew Lot and family were saved from the destruction of Sodom and Gomorrah after Abraham prayed to God saying, Will thou also destroy the righteous with the wicked? That be far from thee to do after this manner, to slay the righteous with the wicked and that the righteous should be as the wicked, that be far from thee: Shall not the Judge of all the earth do right? (Genesis 18:25)

➢ Rahab's faith and righteous actions saved her and her family during Israel's destruction of Jericho. (Joshua 6:25)

➢ God warned Pharaoh and sent plagues on Egypt using his servant Moses while the Israelites were protected and unaffected by them. God brought Israel out, and they crossed safely in the sea, but the Egyptians were drowned. (Exodus chapter 14)

➢ Jeremiah, the prophet, warned backslidden Israel about King Nebuchadnezzar of Babylon. Those who listened to his instructions and surrendered were spared, and those who refused experienced God's judgement - famine and death. (Jeremiah chapter 39)

- ➤ The messenger John, in Revelations, warns the end-time church of being ready for Christ return. Those who do not repent and prepare themselves will suffer loss. Those ready at His return will be rewarded. (Revelations 3:3)

God always warns man before He does anything. He says He does nothing in the earth without revealing it to his prophets (Amos 3:7). His warnings reaffirm how just He is, so that man is without excuse when they are judged by Him. Today, He is speaking through his true prophets telling the world to repent and turn away from this crooked world and turn to Him before destruction comes. This message is not new it has been part of the gospel since the beginning:

> *Save yourselves from this crooked generation.*
> 
> *Acts 2:40*

*Come out from among them, and be separate, and touch not the unclean thing and I will receive you.*

2 Corinthians 6:17

*Come out of her, my people, that ye be not partakers of her sins, and that ye receive not of her plagues.*

Revelations 18:4

*If you will listen to the voice of the Lord thy God, and will do that which is right in his sight, and will give heed to his commandments, and do all his laws, I will put none of these diseases upon you, which I have brought upon the Egyptians.*

Exodus 15:26

*Repent for the kingdom of heaven is at hand –*

Matthew 3:2

*That you may be blameless and harmless, the Sons of God, without rebuke,*

> *in the midst of a crooked and perverse nation, among whom ye shine as lights in the world.* –
>
> *Philippians 2:15*

The scripture says, "Believe His prophets and succeed." (2 Chronicles 20:20) Judah thought Jeremiah was crazy before Babylon came and destroyed their place. His call was heart-wrenching. He stood alone. He was persecuted. He saw the devastation coming, and the people dismissed his warnings, and there was nothing else he could do.

Lot's son-in-laws saw his warnings and advice as a funny joke and not to be taken seriously before they perished in the destruction of Sodom. Many people will choose death instead of humbling and turning themselves over to King Jesus. But that doesn't have to be you. Many may not make it in, but you can be one of the ones who does.

As in the days of Noah, so it will be when the son of man comes, so the scripture says. People will be doing life like always, totally unaware of what will befall them. Like a thief in the night, He will appear. Know that God is ready and able to save all to bring them into His kingdom, but broad is the road to destruction and many go and narrow is the way to life, and few go. It appears very few seemed to be listening then and it's the same today as the call goes out.

I believe, just like we see in scripture, one of the ways God speaks to man is through dreams and visions. As I have heard and been blessed by others who have shared their dreams and experiences, I totally believe this to be true. Over the years, I have had a series of impactful dreams that I believe were from God warning me of what is to come.

In one dream, I was walking along the beach near the water and I could see a massive amount of water coming toward the shore that was over 100 feet high. I was running up and down the shore telling people what was coming, but nobody seemed to see it and nobody seemed to care. It wasn't until it hit where everyone was, that people realized it. I saw it topple many buildings and structures as it made its way on the city streets. It felt extremely real and left me shaken.

In another dream, I found myself alone in my car in a horrific traffic jam that seemed to last for hours without anyone moving forward. I finally proceeded to get out of my car and look ahead to see if I could see what was going on. Upon looking, I saw a huge fireball about a mile high and wide coming towards us from a short distance wiping out everything and everyone in its path. I barely had time to do anything as it was coming so fast. I decided to run toward the side of the road into the bushes with futile hope of getting out of the way, and I awoke abruptly.

The dream seemed so real and scared me so, that upon waking, I immediately fell on my knees in prayer saying, Lord I don't know what that was, but I pray against this disaster I saw. It was during this prayer that I heard the Lord speak to me and say, "Do not pray against the inevitable, just make sure you are ready." I then turned my prayer request toward humbling myself and repenting of any sins before the Lord.

Today I offer you the only hope there is. I have dedicated my life to bringing people to the King, and His Kingdom and to prepare the church to meet their Savior, Lord, and King. It is time to stop fighting for our own kingdom and relinquish all our rights to Him while there is still time. Repentance doesn't seem like a gift from God until it is no longer made available. God gives time; then, time is over. There is no time to lose and no more time to waste. Time is almost up. It is about time for King Jesus to reign fully on the earth as He already does in Heaven. My question is, Will you be a part of this everlasting Kingdom?

www.ingramcontent.com/pod-product-compliance
Lightning Source LLC
Chambersburg PA
CBHW050558300426
44112CB00013B/1974